SECOND HELPINGS

SECOND HELPINGS

by

Johnnie Gabriel

with photography by RON MANVILLE

and food styling by LIBBIE SUMMERS

THOMAS NELSON
Since 1798

NASHVILLE   DALLAS   MEXICO CITY   RIO DE JANEIRO

Published in Nashville, Tennessee, by Thomas Nelson. Thomas Nelson is a registered trademark of Thomas Nelson, Inc.

Photos by Ron Manville

Food styling by Libbie Summers

Thomas Nelson, Inc., titles may be purchased in bulk for educational, business, fund-raising, or sales promotional use. For information, please e-mail SpecialMarkets@ThomasNelson.com.

Library of Congress Control Number: 2010934161

ISBN: 978-1-4016-0001-3

Printed in the United States of America

10 11 12 13 14 QG 6 5 4 3 2

Contents

FOREWORD

I'm blowin' a big kiss to my talented Marietta cousin Johnnie Gabriel for this, her second wonderful cookbook. It doesn't surprise me one bit that she's written a "second helping" of scrumptious recipes from her popular restaurant, Gabriel's. I know a little about cooking, and Johnnie's food will keep you coming back for more, just as it keeps her faithful clientele coming back to Gabriel's day after day.

Those two little words "second helpings" hold so much meaning. Y'all know what I'm talking about? To a cook, they almost seem like coded messages. Asking for second helpings means that your food is good—real good. Good enough to hold your plate out and ask for more. Good enough for the kids to fight over the last serving. Good enough that there is nothing left on the plates when you take them back to the kitchen—they will surely be licked clean. And best of all, good enough that your family, friends, and guests will ask you for the recipe.

The food included in this cookbook comprises those extra-special recipes. Johnnie has time- and taste-tested each and every one, and they've gotten the "second-helping approval stamp" many times over. She has lovingly collected the compliments to share with you in each of these yummy dishes.

And Johnnie knows Southern tastes, too. You can tell by the ingredients that keep showing up: tomatoes, pecans, sweet potatoes, cornbread, and pork. Here's a little clue: You're not eatin' Southern if there aren't at least two or three of these on your plate, Honey! Of course, I'm also willing to bet that you're gonna love Johnnie's Crown Pork Roast with Maple and Cranberry Rice, Tomato and Mozzarella Pie, and Sweet Potato Bread Pudding even if you're not from the South.

Now, go ahead and treat yourself to second helpings. You deserve it, Hon!

—PAULA DEEN

INTRODUCTION

I am so excited and happy to bring you *Second Helpings*. After writing the first cookbook, *Cooking in the South with Johnnie Gabriel,* and the comments I heard from folks who love to cook, just as I do, I knew there were more great recipes I should put in print. I heard from folks who came into Gabriel's for a meal or a dessert: "The creamed corn recipe tastes just like my grandmother [or mother or Aunt Ginny] used to make!" Others remarked that they liked the recipes because they didn't call for a long list of unfamiliar ingredients. Most often, the ingredients are items you normally have in your pantry.

As a person who loves to entertain and takes pride in what I serve my guests, I have a large number of recipes that my husband, Ed, and I have prepared at home. Combined with recipes for the desserts and savory dishes that Gabriel's

Desserts prepares daily, I have a cookbook full of recipes. Thus, *Cooking in the South* was born.

Now here I am with *Second Helpings* and more delicious dishes to cook. It is full of scrumptious recipes because there are a lot of great Marietta cooks, both men and women, who love to entertain. I was able to include only a few . . . I hardly scratched the surface because all the contributors' recipe boxes were full of good things I didn't want to ignore. With every generation there are recipes that should be passed on to the next generation; dishes that we may not necessarily use every week but that provide such great enjoyment for the family when they are prepared. For example, recipes for Red Velvet, Italian Cream, and Hummingbird cakes that Mary Moon shared with me in 1989.

Mary Moon was the "cake lady" of Marietta for many years until she decided it was time to retire. Many might think it coincidental that I needed to earn a few extra dollars about the time Mary was retiring and she graciously shared her recipes with me. I, however, know there are no coincidences in my life. God's hand is working in all good things that come my way, and me sitting in Mary Moon's kitchen one day writing down the recipes for cakes she had made Mariettans for years, myself included, was no coincidence. Here I am—twenty-one years and thousands of cakes later—with the opportunity to share delicious recipes with you, just as Mary Moon shared with me.

Southerners still enjoy a reputation of being hospitable. As far as I can tell, it might have begun right here in Marietta, Georgia. This great town has been my home now for forty-three years and any reason to get together with friends or family for a meal is seized with great fervor. For many of us looking for a new dish to cook, the recipe boxes come out, we scour magazines and the Internet, or best of all we call a friend for the recipe of a dish we enjoyed at her house. The pursuit of looking for the best new dish never ends, just as shopping for the outfit that will make us look five pounds thinner is ongoing. We all believe that dish or dress is just over the horizon.

After the invitations are issued and the shopping and cooking are done, we sit around the table and spend a few minutes discussing the pros and cons and perhaps how we might prepare the food differently and where we might share it next. I don't want to insinuate that food is the only topic of conversation around the tables that I frequent, but the topic is held in high esteem. We are just as curious about who is happily getting married and who is sadly getting divorced, who is expecting a baby and who has died, who is looking for a new job and who is retiring, whether high heels or flats are in, what's the hot new color for the next season and what church is looking for a new preacher. Oftentimes we take the conversation back again to food when we talk excitedly about a new restaurant that is opening.

When a topic consumes that much of your social conversation you've got to know that it's an important subject.

I have had so many fantastic dishes at other cooks' houses and events that I knew there was a wealth of recipes out there that needed to be chronicled and shared. I approached friends, young and old; professional chefs and want-to-be chefs—anyone interested in good food. I asked for their best recipes and they gladly shared.

Also, I'm not saying that you have to be a great cook to love to entertain, because I have recipes in *Second Helpings* from talented caterers. Caterers who have earned their living for many years making other folks' tables look good! What better recipes could there be for me to share with you?

I hope cooking the dishes in *Second Helpings* and sharing them with your family and friends brings you as much joy as I experienced during the time I spent with others gathering and preparing the recipes to bring to you.

—JOHNNIE GABRIEL

Not My Plan

*I*f you had told me twenty years ago that I would own a restaurant serving 350 to 450 people a day, I would have told you that you didn't know me very well. I was comfortable in the role of restaurant patron—one being served, not one serving. Funny how things happen.

And that's not to say my life has always been on a smooth, paved path. I have been a widow, a single mother, and been affected by economic crises. If you are interested in my story in detail, please see *Cooking in the South*, my first cookbook.

I was perfectly happy as a mom with two daughters working hard in school and heading off to college. I had parented and cajoled them over the years to keep them on the straight and narrow and was about to enjoy the freedom of an empty nester. I had also spent years honing my tennis game, teaching Sunday school, and working with the youth in my church. To add to an already full life, I discovered that I loved gardening as much as playing tennis.

I wasn't planning on living a totally self-centered life, and my heart turned toward young, single mothers working to support their families and struggling to find affordable, quality day care. I held an organizational meeting for a Christian-based day care center for low-income parents. I believed the community was to partner with neighbors who needed a helping hand.

A recession in the late '80s, early '90s, pulled me from the tennis court and the garden to a part-time job . . . followed by a full-time job and baking at night. My youngest daughter, Laura, who had been a free-spirited freshman at the University of Georgia, by the middle of her sophomore year no longer had time or money for her sorority. She worked two part-time jobs along with going to school. Both of us were yanked out of our comfort zones. It felt as if I was in the middle of a nightmare.

As I look back down the road we have traveled, I wonder what I would be doing had I continued on the course I had plotted out for myself. I wouldn't have a clue about remaining competitive with the restaurant down the street and at the same time maintaining a profit. (Profitable enough to provide jobs for thirty to forty people.) I would know nothing about hiring the mentally challenged and how hard many of them work to overcome their disabilities. I now understand what it adds to the self-esteem of an individual when someone hands him or her a check at the end of the week and says, "Thanks! Job well done!" And it truly gives me a sense of accomplishment to serve someone a steaming plate of country fried steak and vegetables, then bus the table, thank the customer, and wipe down the table for the next customer.

It probably sounds as though I had never worked a day in my life before owning a restaurant or that I had never intended to work—but I did. I worked during high school, and after I was married I worked during the day and attended night classes. All with one goal in mind—to set our family up for me to be a stay-at-home mom, as my mother was never able to be. Here I am, forty years later, and the Lord has organized my life to experience the best of both worlds. His planning is so much better than mine!

Nothing makes me happier than spending time with Stephanie (left) and Laura (right)!

Tom and Libbie working diligently to get the perfect shot for us. See the result on page 10.

APPETIZERS

CHEDDAR HAM CUPS

This recipe is from Dot Downing, a Sunday school class member. When Dot makes these we can count on our bodies and souls being fed on Sunday morning. You might want to make a double batch, because they disappear quickly.

. . . .

1	tube (10.2 ounces) large refrigerated flaky biscuits	2	packages (2¹/2 ounces each) thinly sliced deli ham, chopped
2	cups (8 ounces) finely shredded cheddar cheese	3/4	cup mayonnaise
		1/3	cup real bacon bits
		2 to 3	teaspoons Dijon mustard

. . . .

Preheat the oven to 450 degrees.

Horizontally split the biscuits into thirds, peeling the layers apart. Press one layer into the bottom and up the side of each ungreased miniature muffin cup and set aside while you prepare the filling.

In a medium bowl combine the cheddar cheese, deli ham, mayonnaise, bacon bits, and Dijon mustard. Fill each biscuit with about 1 tablespoon of cheese mixture.

Bake at 450 degrees for 9 to 11 minutes, or until golden brown and the cheese is melted. Let stand for 2 minutes before removing from the pans. Serve warm.

Makes 2¹/2 dozen.

Caramelized Onion and Mushroom Rolls

Adapted from "Come on In" recipes from the Junior League of Jackson, Mississippi cookbook. My Sunday school class loved these when I made them. They are often guinea pigs for my recipe testing.

2	packages crescent dinner rolls		1/2	teaspoon seasoned salt
1 to 2	tablespoons olive oil		1/2	teaspoon tarragon
1/3	cup sweet onion, chopped		1	egg, beaten
1	(8-ounce) package cream cheese, room temperature			poppy seeds
1	(4-ounce) can mushrooms, stems and pieces, drained and chopped			

Preheat the oven to 375 degrees. Lay out the crescent roll dough and press the perforations to seal.

In a small sauté pan heat the olive oil over medium heat and add the onions. Sauté until caramelized and golden in color (about 15 minutes). Drain the onions on a paper towel to absorb the oil. Cool.

In a mixing bowl, thoroughly combine the cream cheese, mushrooms, onions, salt, and tarragon. Spread over the dough all the way to the edges.

From the long side of the pastry, roll up jelly roll-style. If the dough has become too warm to hold its shape, refrigerate it for 30 minutes prior to slicing with a serrated knife into 3/4- to 1-inch pieces. Reshape the dough into a circle if necessary after cutting, and place on a cookie sheet 1- to 1 1/2-inches apart. Brush the top and sides with the beaten egg. Sprinkle with poppy seeds.

The rolls may be prepared ahead to this point and frozen or covered with plastic wrap and held in the refrigerator for a couple of hours before baking. Overnight refrigeration inhibits the rising of the dough when baked.

Bake 10 to 12 minutes or until lightly browned. Serve hot.

Makes 24 rolls.

CHICKEN, GOAT CHEESE, AND CRANBERRY WRAP

I served these at Taste of Atlanta, where they were a huge hit! Serve these at your next party, ladies luncheon, or tailgating event. They'd also make a great after-school snack.

1   (11-ounce) package goat cheese
1/4   cup chopped walnuts, lightly toasted
2   tablespoons honey
1/3   cup Craisins, chopped
2   tablespoons whole berry cranberry sauce

1   (14-ounce) package lavash flat bread *
12   ounces sliced deli maple glazed chicken or roasted chicken
1/2   cup spinach leaves or arugula

Preheat the oven to 350 degrees.

Lay the goat cheese out for about 15 minutes prior to mixing so that it softens a bit. Meanwhile, lightly toast the chopped walnuts on a baking sheet in the oven for 4 to 8 minutes. Stir halfway through to toast evenly.

In a medium bowl use an electric mixer to beat the goat cheese and honey. Add the walnuts, Craisins, and 2 tablespoons cranberry sauce and mix with a spatula.

Place three pieces of the flat bread on a baking sheet and heat in the oven for 3 to 5 minutes, just enough to soften the bread for rolling. Remove the bread from the oven and when it is just cool enough to handle, spread the goat cheese mixture over the bread to the 4 edges. Cover the goat cheese with the chicken slices and spinach.

Starting on the long side of the bread (if there is one longer than the other), tightly roll up the bread, jelly roll-style. The goat cheese spread will seal the rolls. Wrap the rolls in plastic wrap and place them seam side down and refrigerate for 2 to 3 hours or overnight. When ready to serve, unwrap and slice into 3/8-inch or 1/2-inch slices. Skewer them horizontally with a toothpick to serve.

Refrigerate any leftovers.

Makes 48 to 72 pieces.

TIP: This recipe can easily be prepared up to twenty-four hours ahead of time.

* Flat bread can be found in the deli section of your grocery store. It is typically 8 x 8 1/2-inches.

MEDITERRANEAN CHEESE SPREAD DIP

Growing up in the South and in a Greek household, Mary Miltiades got a double dose of the love for preparation and serving of good food. Her mom and dad, Dee and Evans Nichols, loved to entertain and show the rest of us the magic of the Greek touch added to a dish. Mary sure inherited that talent and then embellished on it. She caters a lot of parties and is often catering right up until Christmas Eve. Then she prepares a huge Christmas meal for family, friends, and anybody else she finds out doesn't have another place to be on Christmas Day. This cheese spread will make you want to be on Mary's guest list!

5	(8-ounce) packages cream cheese, softened	1	(6-ounce) jar sundried tomatoes in oil, drained and chopped
8	eggs	1	(14-ounce) can artichoke hearts, drained and chopped
1/2	pound feta cheese		
3/4	cup Parmesan cheese	1	bunch green onions, chopped (white and green portions)
2	tablespoons dried parsley		
2	teaspoons garlic powder	1	stick butter, melted
1	tablespoon dried basil	1	(1/2-pound) box phyllo dough
1	tablespoon dried oregano		Fresh parsley, for garnish

Preheat the oven to 350 degrees.

In a large bowl beat the cream cheese with an electric mixer until creamy. Add the eggs and beat until smooth. Add the feta and parmesan cheeses, the parsley, garlic powder, basil, and oregano. Blend in the tomatoes, artichokes, and green onions. Set aside.

Using a pastry brush dipped in melted butter, butter 5 to 6 sheets of phyllo and fold each in half. Drape each sheet over the side of a 9-inch springform pan, overlapping all the way around. Butter 2 to 3 sheets and fold in half to cover the bottom. Butter 5 to 6 sheets and fold in half. Put the sheets up the sides and in the bottom. Butter 4 to 6 sheets and fold in thirds and place around the sides. Fold the draped sheets back over to seal the "crust."

Pour the cream cheese mixture into the phyllo crust. Bake $1^{1}/4$ to $1^{1}/2$ hours or until golden brown on top. The sides of the top will crack when done. Garnish with fresh parsley sprigs and serve with toast rounds or pita chips.

Serves 60 to 70.

BLACK-EYED PEA SPREAD

Gail Ré, my good friend and talented artist, gave me this recipe. Gail has played an integral role in my life and Gabriel's Desserts over the years. She not only encourages me, but also used her amazing artistic ability to guide the decorating both times Gabriel's has expanded.

1	large Vidalia onion, chopped	1	(16-ounce) can black-eyed peas
2	tablespoons butter	1	(16-ounce) can black beans,
1/2	cup sour cream		drained and rinsed
1/2	cup mayonnaise	1	(14-ounce) can artichokes,
1	envelope dry Ranch salad		drained and chopped
	dressing mix	2	cups shredded mozzarella cheese

Preheat the oven to 350 degrees.

In a medium skillet sauté the onion in butter until tender.

In a medium bowl whisk together the sour cream, mayonnaise, and dressing mix. Gently fold in the peas, beans, and artichokes. Add the sautéed onions and spoon the mixture into an 11-inch round baking dish or any dish of comparable size that has been sprayed with a nonstick spray.

Bake for 20 to 25 minutes. Sprinkle with the cheese and bake an additional 10 minutes or until bubbly. Serve with the crackers of your choice.

Serves 8 to 10.

TIP: This dip is especially good when served with sesame crackers.

BLACK BEAN AND FETA DIP

Black beans are so healthy and just one of my favorite comfort foods. Lindy Jones has combined them with one of my other favorite flavors . . . feta cheese. Enjoy another convenient and easy dip for family or entertaining from Lindy.

2	(11-ounce) cans shoepeg corn, drained	1/2	cup sugar
2	(15-ounce) cans black beans, rinsed and drained	1/2	cup apple cider vinegar
		1/2	cup olive oil
1	bunch green onions, chopped	4	ounces feta cheese
2	Roma tomatoes, peeled, seeded, and chopped		chopped cilantro, optional

In a medium bowl combine the corn, beans, green onions, tomatoes, sugar, vinegar, oil, feta cheese, and cilantro. Place in the refrigerator to marinate for up to one day before serving. Serve with tortilla chips.

Serves 10 to 12.

BRUSCHETTA CUPS

Another good recipe from Liz Cole.

1	pint grape tomatoes, chopped and drained	1	clove garlic, halved
5	fresh basil leaves, chiffonade*	1	teaspoon olive oil
4	ounces part-skim mozzarella cheese		salt and freshly ground pepper to taste
		30	phyllo cups, prebaked

In a small bowl, toss the chopped tomatoes with the basil leaves. Slice the cheese into 1/4-inch slices and rub both sides of each slice with the cut edge of the garlic half. Dice the cheese slices into little cubes and toss with the tomatoes. Stir in the olive oil; season to taste with salt and pepper.

Spoon 1 teaspoon of the tomato mixture into each phyllo cup. Serve immediately.

Makes 30 pieces.

* See glossary on page 267.

Beef Tataki*

One thing in life that Southerners pride themselves on is our appreciation of good food. Tom McEachern serves this very special appetizer at Ray's on the River. This is not exactly a Southern recipe, but it is good food.

1   (5-ounce) hanger steak
2   teaspoons blackening seasoning
2   teaspoons olive oil
1   cup balsamic vinegar pomegranate-flavored syrup or a balsamic vinegar reduction**

1/2 to 1 cup micro greens or any small chopped greens
2 to 3 ounces thinly sliced Reggiano cheese
1   pomegranate, cut in half and seeds removed***
    sea salt for garnish (optional)

Dry the steak with paper towels and evenly and thoroughly rub the blackening seasoning all over the steak. Rub all sides with the olive oil. Heat a dry, cast-iron skillet on high to very hot temperature, hot enough to quickly sear the meat 30 to 45 seconds on each side and the ends, forming a "crust" on the meat. The center will still be cool. Thinly slice the meat and place on the serving plate. Drizzle the sliced steak with the balsamic syrup. Scatter the greens over the top, along with several pieces of the cheese. Scatter pomegranate seeds over the greens and meat. If desired, lightly scatter sea salt over the meat. Serve with small, thinly sliced bread or crackers.

Serves 2 to 3.

ALTERNATE COOKING METHOD: You can sear the meat over a hot grill instead, if you prefer.

---

 * *Tataki* is a method of preparing fish or meat in Japanese cuisine. It is seared very briefly over a hot flame or pan and served thinly sliced.

** Balsamic vinegar reduction: Use 3 to 4 times the amount of vinegar you want the process to yield. One cup of balsamic vinegar simmered in a saucepan until reduced by about 75 percent yields 3 to 4 tablespoons. The vinegar is ready when the mixture coats the back of a spoon.

*** To remove the seeds from the pomegranate, cut the fruit in half and hold over a bowl. With the back of a wooden spoon, tap the outside skin of the fruit until the seeds begin to fall out.

CHEESE AND APPLE SPREAD

When I was a child, my mom melted a slice of cheddar cheese on top of my dad's piece of apple pie. I gave my own children apples and cheese for a snack. But I had never put apples and cream cheese in an appetizer together until Liz Cole brought this unusual combination to our Sunday school class. Guess what? Mixed all together, they really complement one another.

1 (8-ounce) package cream cheese, softened	1 cup shredded sharp cheddar cheese
1 cup mayonnaise	1 cup finely chopped apple, with peel, (1 large apple)

In a medium bowl, mix the cream cheese, mayonnaise, cheddar cheese, and apple together. Refrigerate until ready to serve.

Serve with apple slices or Triscuits.

Serves 6.

NOTE: Use low-fat cream cheese and/or mayonnaise if you like.

TIP: If you have the time to make this the day before, the flavors will develop nicely.

SHRIMP SPREAD

This is such a good appetizer and so easy to put together at the last minute.

1/2	cup margarine or butter, softened		1	small onion, finely chopped
1	(8-ounce) package cream cheese		1/2	cup chopped celery
2	teaspoons mayonnaise			dash of salt and pepper
1	teaspoon Worcestershire sauce		2	cups small shrimp, cooked and
2	teaspoons lemon juice			drained*

In a medium bowl combine the butter, cream cheese, mayonnaise, Worcestershire sauce, lemon juice, onion, celery, and salt and pepper. Mix until smooth. Add the shrimp and stir.

Serve with crackers.

Serves 6 to 8.

* This recipe also works well with leftover shrimp. Just make sure to chop it up.

CHEESE TIDBITS

Claire Francis, a good friend and tennis buddy, shared this recipe with me. The consistency is like a cheese straw, but this doesn't have cayenne pepper. It has sugar. You'll want to share this with all of your friends.

1/2 pound sharp cheddar cheese, grated	1/2 cup confectioners' sugar, sifted
	1/2 cup pecans, chopped
1/2 pound (2 sticks) butter, softened	3 cups sifted all-purpose flour

In a mixing bowl combine the cheese, butter, sugar, pecans, and flour. Mix well with a spatula or wooden spoon. Shape into a log and wrap in waxed paper. Refrigerate at least an hour before slicing.

Preheat the oven to 350 degrees. Slice the cheese into 1/4-inch slices and place on a cookie sheet. Bake 10 minutes, or until lightly browned.

Makes 48.

CHEESE WAFERS WITH A TWIST

Mary Gillis took Paula Deen's recipe for Pecan–Date Cheese Wafers and added sausage and some brown sugar. What a delicious twist! This is an example of starting with a great recipe, tweaking it, and making it your own!

1/4 cup light brown sugar	1/2 teaspoon ground red pepper
1 1/2 cups butter, softened	4 1/4 cups all-purpose flour
1 pound sharp cheddar cheese, finely grated	1 pound sausage, browned and drained
1 cup finely chopped pecans	turbinado sugar
1 cup finely chopped dates	

In a large mixing bowl use an electric mixer to beat the brown sugar with the butter until well blended. Add the cheese, pecans, dates, and red pepper. Beat at medium speed until well combined. Gradually add the flour, beating until just combined. Add the sausage and mix thoroughly. Wrap the dough in plastic wrap and refrigerate for 2 hours.

Preheat the oven to 350 degrees. Line baking sheets with parchment paper. Pinch off portions of the dough to roll into 1-inch round pieces and place the balls 3 inches apart on the prepared baking sheet. Using a flat-bottomed glass or your fingers dipped in flour, flatten the balls to 1/4-inch thickness. Sprinkle turbinado sugar on top and bake for 10 to 12 minutes, or until lightly browned. Let the wafers cool on the pans for 2 minutes. Place the wafers on cooling racks and allow them to cool completely. Store in an airtight container in the freezer for up to 30 days. Bring to room temperature when ready to serve.

Makes 9 dozen.

LAYERED CHEESE TERRINE

This hors d'oeuvre is one of my favorites. It is not inexpensive and it does require preplanning, but it is so worth it. Two very good cooks, Betty Burnside and Cindy Dye, contributed this recipe. They keep it in the "favorites" section of their collection and serve it on special occasions in their home.

1/4 cup butter
1 (8-ounce) package cream cheese, softened
1 clove garlic
1/2 cup pistachios, rough chopped
1 pound provolone cheese, thinly sliced, divided

1 cup pesto, purchased or homemade
1/2 cup oil-packed sundried tomatoes, chopped and divided

thinly sliced baguette or crackers

In a mixing bowl or in a food processor, combine the butter and cream cheese and blend. Add the garlic and blend again. Fold in the pistachios (I like the texture of the chopped pistachios instead of pureeing them in the processor with the cream cheese). Set aside.

Line a 4 x 8-inch loaf pan with waxed paper. Place a layer of provolone on the bottom and around the sides and end of the pan, slightly overlapping each slice.

Spread 1/2 cup pesto over the cheese and place another layer of provolone over the pesto.

Sprinkle half of the chopped tomatoes over the provolone and spread the garlic mixture over the tomatoes.

Sprinkle the remaining tomatoes over the garlic mixture.

Add another layer of provolone over the tomatoes. Spread the remaining pesto over the provolone and finish with a final layer of provolone. You should have 9 separate layers when finished.

Fold the provolone over the top to seal. Tap the loaf pan on the counter to settle the terrine. Fold the waxed paper over the dish to cover the cheese. If the waxed paper doesn't cover the cheese, add a piece of plastic wrap. Lay a brick on top of the terrine to press the ingredients together. The terrine should be made at least one day in advance. Serve with thinly sliced baguette or crackers.

Serves 12 to 18.

NOTE: Terrine can mean an earthenware dish for cooking or, when used loosely, can be applied to the food that is prepared therein. A terrine is merely components of a recipe that are layered in an oblong dish and pressed together for a time. This dish is then turned out onto a plate and served in slices. The components not only make a colorful presentation but are delicious to eat.

When complete this dish will have one layer of garlic cream, two layers of sundried tomatoes, two of pesto, and four layers of cheese. If you get some of the components out of order, no harm done, as long as you begin and end with cheese.

TIP: If you don't have a brick you can use a bag of sugar wrapped in plastic wrap.

SUZY'S BAKED CORN APPETIZER

I have enjoyed this appetizer often but never knew what gave the dish so much flavor until Marcelle David shared the recipe with me for **Second Helpings.** *This is one of the first dishes to go at events I have attended. I'll bet your guests come back for second helpings.*

1	(11-ounce) can Mexican corn, drained	1	cup shredded Monterey Jack cheese
1	(4-ounce) jar pimientos, drained	1/2	cup shredded Parmesan cheese
2	ounces jalapeño peppers, finely chopped	1	cup mayonnaise tortilla chips

Preheat the oven to 350 degrees.

In a medium bowl combine the corn, pimientos, peppers, cheeses, and mayonnaise with a spatula or wooden spoon. Turn into a greased baking dish and bake for 30 minutes.

Serve with tortilla chips.

Serves 8.

FRIED OKRA, TEMPURA-STYLE

Our friend Tom McEachern, executive chef of Ray's on the River restaurant here in Atlanta, created one of the most interesting appetizers I've seen: Southern fried okra with an Asian dipping sauce. Southern fried okra is one of the most popular dishes we serve at Gabriel's. I bet you'll love Tom's version too!

	vegetable oil (for frying)	1	quart soda water
2	cups all-purpose flour	1	pound fresh whole okra pods,
3/4	cup plus 2 tablespoons cornstarch		washed and drained
1/4	teaspoon baking soda		Mae Ploy Sweet Chili dipping
1/8	teaspoon cayenne pepper		sauce*

Add the vegetable oil to a large skillet or Dutch oven and heat it to 375 degrees.

In a medium bowl combine the flour, cornstarch, baking soda, and cayenne pepper. Pour the soda water into the bowl and stir only until incorporated, leaving some small lumps.

Dip the okra pods in the batter. Gently shake off excess batter and place in the oil. Fry until golden brown. Serve with Mae Ploy sauce.

Serves 6 as an appetizer.

TIP: Don't stir the batter too much or it will become tough.

* You can find Mae Ploy Sweet Chili dipping sauce in the Asian section of most major grocery stores.

MANGO CHUTNEY AND CURRY (OR NOT) CREAM CHEESE SPREAD

To curry or not to curry? My niece, Beth Sharon, brought this to my house for a family gathering but wouldn't take the leftovers home because she would eat it all herself. She left it for me to devour, and I did! If you're not a curry fan you can leave it out, but I highly recommend trying it both ways!

1   (8-ounce) package cream cheese, softened
1   teaspoon curry powder
1   (6-ounce) jar mango chutney
1/2 to 3/4 cup grated sharp cheddar cheese

4 to 6 green onions, tops only sliced
4 to 6 slices bacon, cooked and crumbled
1   bag corn chip scoops

In a medium mixing bowl combine the softened cream cheese with the curry powder and spread on the bottom of an 8 x 8-inch serving dish. Spread the chutney over the cream cheese, followed by the cheddar cheese, green onion tops, and the chopped bacon. Serve immediately with the corn chips or refrigerate until ready to serve.

Serves 6 to 8.

TIP: This recipe can be easily doubled for a larger crowd.

THREE-CHEESE MINI MACS HORS D'OEUVRES

You can make most of this recipe ahead of time and refrigerate it. Just finish it off in the oven when you're ready to serve it.

1/2	pound elbow macaroni	1	cup shredded cheddar cheese
1 1/2	tablespoons unsalted butter, plus more for brushing	4	ounces deli-sliced American cheese, chopped
1/4	cup freshly grated Parmigiano-Reggiano cheese	1	large egg yolk
2	tablespoons all-purpose flour	1/4	teaspoon smoked Spanish paprika
3/4	cup milk	1/2	cup finely chopped ham (optional)

Preheat the oven to 425 degrees. In a large saucepan of boiling salted water, cook the macaroni until *al dente* (firm to the bite), about 5 minutes. Drain, shaking off the excess water.

Brush four 12-cup nonstick mini muffin tins with melted butter. Evenly sprinkle 2 tablespoons of the Parmigiano-Reggiano into the forty-eight cups; tap out the excess.

In a large saucepan, melt the 1 1/2 tablespoons of butter. Whisk in the flour over moderate heat for 2 minutes. Whisk in the milk and cook, whisking, until boiling, about 5 minutes. Add the cheddar and American cheeses and whisk until melted. Remove from the heat and whisk in the egg yolk and paprika. Fold in the macaroni and ham, if using.

Spoon slightly rounded tablespoons of the macaroni into the prepared muffin cups, packing them gently. Evenly sprinkle the remaining 2 tablespoons of Parmigiano-Reggiano on top.

Bake the mini macs in the upper and middle thirds of the oven for about 10 minutes, until golden and sizzling. Let cool for 5 minutes. Using a small spoon, carefully loosen them and transfer to a platter. Serve hot.

Makes 48 pieces. Serves 12 as an appetizer.

MARY'S BRIE
WITH CHUTNEY AND PISTACHIOS

Please, can somebody tell me a dish that bacon doesn't make taste better? Another winner here . . . just don't overheat.

1   (13 1/2-ounce) brie wheel, cut in half horizontally
1   (9-ounce) bottle Major Grey's chutney

3/4 to 1 cup chopped pistachios
10 to 12 ounces bacon, cooked and crumbled
crackers or thinly sliced bread

Preheat the oven to 350 degrees.

Place the bottom half of the brie in an ovenproof dish. Generously spread the chutney over the brie. Top with pistachios and crumbled bacon. Replace the top half of the brie and repeat the chutney, and bacon layers.

Heat in the oven just until the brie begins to melt. Serve with your favorite cracker or thinly sliced bread.

Serves 6.

MEDITERRANEAN
BLACK AND WHITE BEAN SALSA

This is just delicious. I have made this recipe forever. It is so flavorful, colorful, and refreshing in the summer.

4	tablespoons corn oil, divided	3	tablespoons fresh lime juice
1¼	cups fresh corn kernels or frozen, thawed	3	large cloves garlic, pressed
1	(16-ounce) can black beans, drained and rinsed	1	large jalapeño, seeded and minced
1	(15-ounce) can Great Northern beans, drained	1	tablespoon minced fresh oregano (1 teaspoon dried)
1	cup chopped red pepper	1	tablespoon chili powder
3/4	cup chopped red onion	1½	teaspoons ground cumin
			salt and pepper, to taste

In a heavy skillet heat 2 tablespoons of oil over high heat. Add the corn and sauté about 3 minutes until brown. Place the sautéed corn in a large bowl. Add the remaining 2 tablespoons of oil, the black and Great Northern beans, red pepper, red onion, lime juice, garlic, jalapeño, oregano, chili powder, and ground cumin. Stir to combine with a spatula or wooden spoon. Season to taste with salt and pepper. Store covered in the refrigerator for up to two days.

Makes 1 quart.

NOTE: Prepare and refrigerate at least 4 to 6 hours before serving. This dish is best served at room temperature.

TIP: Serve with tortilla chips, on a salad with chicken or beef, or meatless as a vegetarian dish.

OYSTERS ROCKEFELLER WITH A TWIST

My friends, Cindy and Marshall Dye, both spent part of their childhood in New Orleans, going out to the oyster beds with parents and harvesting the oysters and eating them on the spot or dining in some of New Orleans wonderful restaurants. The Dyes love to travel and to eat oysters so everywhere they go they can be found checking out the Oysters Rockefeller dish if it's on the menu. After years of eating everyone else's, they decided to create their own recipe. This is their rendition and the result of their time spent on the road and in their very own kitchen.

1	box rock salt (ice cream salt)	2	tablespoons minced garlic
1/4	cup water	1	(9-ounce) bag fresh spinach
1	dozen oysters in shell	1	teaspoon salt
	(Gulf or Apalachicola)	1	teaspoon white pepper
1/4	cup butter	2	tablespoons sherry
2	tablespoons finely chopped onion	1	cup Hollandaise sauce

Preheat the oven to 450 degrees. Prepare a roasting pan by filling it 1/2- to 3/4-inch deep with rock salt. Sprinkle the salt with the 1/4 cup water. The salt will stabilize the shell on the pan and help keep the oysters hot.

Clean the oysters under cold running water. Using an oyster shucking knife at the joint of each oyster, insert the blade and twist to open the shell. Cut each oyster at the muscle to separate it from the shell. Place each oyster on the deep half of the shell, and discard the other half. Place oysters on the bed of rock salt.

In a large sauté pan over medium heat melt the butter. Add the onion and garlic and sauté until the onion is tender, being careful not to burn the garlic. Add the spinach, salt, and pepper, and cover to steam the spinach.

Pour 1/2 teaspoon of sherry over each oyster. Spoon 1 tablespoon spinach onto each oyster, followed with enough Hollandaise sauce* to cover the spinach mixture.

Bake for 10 minutes. Switch the oven to broil and cook, keeping careful watch, until the tops of the oysters are brown and bubbling.

Serves 3 to 4 as an appetizer.

*See page 257 for Cindy's Hollandaise sauce recipe.

OYSTERS CINDERELLA

If you check out the Oysters Rockefeller recipe on page 31, you will see it was given to me by Marshall and Cindy Dye. They love oysters, raw or cooked, and have explored many ways to prepare them. They've cooked a lot of them—so many that part of her garden is mulched with oyster shells. Here's one of their favorite recipes other than "Rockefeller."

1	box rock salt (ice cream salt)	1/2	cup shredded Parmesan cheese
1/4	cup water	1/2	teaspoon dry mustard
1	dozen oysters in shells	1/4	cup butter, melted
	(Gulf or Apalachicola)*	4	slices bacon, cooked crisp and
1	cup sour cream		crumbled finely
1/4	cup butter cracker crumbs		

Preheat the oven to 450 degrees. Prepare a roasting pan by filling it 1/2- to 3/4-inch deep with rock salt. Sprinkle the salt with water. The salt will stabilize the shell on the pan and help keep the oysters hot.

Clean the oysters under cold running water. Using an oyster shucking knife at the joint of each oyster, insert the blade and twist to open the shell. Cut each oyster at the muscle to separate it from the shell. Place each oyster on the deep half of the shell, and discard the other half. Place oysters on the bed of rock salt.

Spoon 1 teaspoon of sour cream onto each oyster.

In a small bowl mix cracker crumbs, Parmesan cheese, and dry mustard. Add the butter and mix well.

Spoon about 2 teaspoons of cheese mixture over the sour cream on each oyster. Top with bacon crumbles.

Cook for 10 minutes until bubbly and brown on top. If the crumble mixture doesn't brown, switch the oven to broil and cook very briefly until brown.

Serves 3 or 4 as an appetizer.

*When purchasing oysters, ask when the oysters were harvested. Try to cook oysters within five days of their harvest.

SOUTH MEETS WEST
BLACK-EYED PEA DIP

This little appetizer is so simple to make and so good. Just what Lindy Jones, my godchild, mother of two, and carpool specialist, needs. She can keep the ingredients in her pantry and whip up an appetizer for last-minute occasions.

1   (15-ounce) can black-eyed peas, drained
1   (14.5-ounce) can white corn, drained
1   (14.5-ounce) can diced tomatoes
1   (10-ounce) can Rotel diced tomatoes with chilies

1   green pepper, chopped
    chopped cilantro to taste
1   (14 to 16 ounce) bottle Italian dressing
    garlic salt to taste
    salt and pepper to taste

In a medium bowl mix the black-eyed peas, corn, tomatoes, green pepper, cilantro, Italian dressing, garlic salt, and salt and pepper, combining well. Marinate in the refrigerator for a few hours or up to one day before serving.

Serve with tortilla chips.

Serves 12.

Sun-dried Tomato Cheeseball

Liz Cole says this recipe falls into the category of her "sure to garner compliments" group. We discussed the fact that cheeseballs are somewhat thought to be old hat and passed over at the appetizer table these days. If you serve this one, you'll find that your guests linger over it instead of bypassing it.

3 (8-ounce) packages cream cheese, softened	2 teaspoons dried basil
1 (7-ounce) jar oil-packed sundried tomatoes, drained	1 clove garlic, halved
	1/2 cup coarsely chopped almonds or pine nuts, toasted

In the bowl of a food processor equipped with the knife blade, add the cream cheese, sundried tomatoes, basil, and garlic. Process the mixture until smooth, roll into a ball, and then wrap in plastic wrap. Chill thoroughly.

When the mixture is chilled enough to hold its shape, roll the ball in the chopped nuts, pressing the nuts into the ball, and wrap in plastic wrap. Refrigerate up to 5 days.

Serve with unsalted crackers.

Serves 24 to 30.

VARIATION: Omit the nuts and serve the mixture in a bowl as a spread instead.

ALTERNATE SERVING SUGGESTION: Make 3 smaller cheeseballs and leave some without nuts.

LEFTOVER TIP: Any leftover cheeseball can be tossed with hot pasta for a quick sauce.

NOTE: If you do not use a food processor, make sure you chop the sundried tomatoes finely.

NOTE: Pine nuts and almonds burn easily. Keep a close eye on them when toasting.

SWEET AND SALTY ROASTED PECANS

My friend Alexis Edwards Amaden shared this recipe with me. Lexie's family owns the Whitlock Inn here in Marietta. It is a beautiful setting for weddings and receptions. Lots of happy brides and good food from her catering company, Carriage House Catering, occupies Lexie's weekends.

1	teaspoon sugar	1	teaspoon water
1	teaspoon salt	1	egg white, stiffly beaten
1	teaspoon milk	2	cups pecans

Preheat the oven to 300 degrees.

Place the sugar, salt, milk, water, egg white, and pecans in a zip-top bag and shake to coat. Spread the pecans on a foil-lined cookie sheet and bake 15 minutes. With a spatula, turn and stir the pecans to toast the other side. Bake 15 more minutes.

Store in an airtight container.

Makes 2 cups.

TIP: Make a double batch during football season.

FRIENDSHIPS FORGED
IN THE KITCHEN

I have always treasured friendships. Whether it is time spent in a home or restaurant kitchen, on the tennis court, golf course, ball field, at church, work, or on vacation, just about anywhere you spend time with people with whom you have a common interest or a common goal, I think you can find the potential to form strong friendships.

It is amazing the friendships that can be formed when you spend time with people either eating or cooking. My first daughter, Stephanie, taught me this. I was only twenty-one and she was the first baby in our circle of friends. She was as cute and charming as she could be. Everyone wanted to coochy-coo and hold Stephanie, but she was quick to let you know if she considered you "worthy" of her affection. We finally realized when she was about two that the difference in how well Stephanie received someone's attention was directly linked to whether she had shared a meal with that person. Babysitters were few and far between, so Stephanie was normally in her high chair at the table when we ate with friends. Once she had shared a meal with you, she could be your friend.

In the culinary world, I have found that "sharing the load" in a kitchen can turn a coworker into a friend. My warmest memories are of the people who have been there for me during the critical times, times when they "officially" could have

Debbie Goss (left) and Tiffany Hall (right) ready with big smiles for customers.

done their eight hours and gone home, but they chose to stay until the job was finished. That has been true not only in the kitchen at Gabriel's when we were overcommitted but also in my home kitchen when the job of hosting a party became overwhelming.

Gabriel's employees are paid for every hour they work, but sometimes during holidays there is not enough money to compensate for, as my mother used to say, "being bone tired." I have been blessed with people in my professional life who have committed to projects and taken ownership to see them through.

Martha Nicolas in our decorating room.

I know it happens in other professions, but friendly relationships can truly be tested in a kitchen. There's always a deadline. There's the heat. There can be seemingly never-ending cleanup. Mistakes can't be corrected with an eraser or the touch of a button on a keyboard. Many times the only answer is to start over. We have delivered food in the pouring rain, the blistering heat, and in the freezing cold. You become very familiar with each other's temperament in these conditions.

I have forged great friendships carrying

fragile but heavy wedding cakes, coolers loaded with food, and carts of cake-filled boxes up the loading ramps of hotels. I probably won't remember the flavor of cake, but I will remember the faces of the people who shared the load.

If you're looking for a way to forge friendships and make memories, spend time in the kitchen with someone, especially your children. Cooking a dish for the family gives such a sense of accomplishment and self-confidence. Cooking teaches skills that will last a lifetime. I can't think of anyone they'll meet who won't appreciate talent in the kitchen.

Changing or doubling recipes will also give your children an opportunity to work on math skills. On one visit to my daughter's house, I asked my youngest grandson, Heath, to write the grocery list. He was just learning to write, and you should have seen how proud he was when we filled up the grocery cart from his handwritten list. My oldest grandson, Wyatt, has always loved to cook. His dad just spent six months in Afghanistan, and while he was gone, Wyatt was able to do all the grilling for his mom. My granddaughter Laney is just three and a half, so she doesn't do much cooking, but she's in the kitchen when the boys are. She doesn't want to miss a thing her big brothers do. Isn't it great that they are modeling a wholesome, practical skill? Cooking can be a family sport, I'm thinking.

For me, time spent in the kitchen, whether work or play, has made my life better!

Fried Green Tomato and Ripe Red Tomato Salad with Goat Cheese (page 42)

Soups and Salads

Fried Green Tomato and Ripe Red Tomato Salad with Goat Cheese

Ed and I have done cooking demonstrations twice now at the Strand Theater on the Square in Marietta. What a great time we had! One of the shows we did was called "How to Throw a Simple Southern Dinner Party." With enough planning, a dinner party shouldn't be mind-blowing. Good company and good food is a combination that's hard to beat.

Balsamic reduction:
- 2 cups balsamic vinegar
- 2 cloves garlic, minced

Salad:
- 2 large ripe beefsteak or heirloom tomatoes, cored and sliced 1/2-inch thick (about 1 pound)
- 1/2 cup all-purpose flour
- 1/2 cup yellow cornmeal
- 2 tablespoons sugar
- 1 teaspoon salt
- 1/2 teaspoon freshly ground black pepper
- 1/4 teaspoon cayenne pepper

- 1 large egg
- 1/2 cup buttermilk
- 1/2 cup vegetable oil
- 2 tablespoons bacon grease*
- 4 large green tomatoes, cored and sliced 1/2-inch thick
- 1/2 pint grape tomatoes, red or golden variety, halved lengthwise
- 4 ounces goat cheese, crumbled (about 1 cup)
- 8 slices bacon, cooked crisp and crumbled
- 8 fresh basil leaves, cut into thin strips

Make the balsamic reduction: In a saucepan over medium heat combine the vinegar and the garlic and bring to a boil. Reduce the heat to low and continue to simmer until it is reduced to about 1/2 cup.

Make the salad: Preheat the oven to 200 degrees. Line a baking sheet with paper towels. Arrange the ripe tomato slices in one layer on a large platter or on individual plates. Season to taste with salt and freshly ground pepper, and drizzle with the balsamic reduction.

In a shallow pan combine the flour, cornmeal, sugar, 1 teaspoon salt, and black and cayenne pepper.

In a medium bowl whisk the egg and buttermilk together.

Pour enough oil and bacon grease if using, in a large skillet to fill 1/4-inch deep. Heat over medium-high heat to about 375 degrees, or until the oil sizzles when you drop a small amount of flour into the skillet.

Dip a green tomato slice in the egg-buttermilk mixture to coat both sides, dredge it in the flour mixture to coat both sides, and place it in the hot oil. Repeat with enough tomato slices to fill the skillet without crowding and fry until the underside is golden brown, about 2 minutes. Turn and fry the other side to golden brown. Use tongs or a slotted spatula to transfer the fried tomato slices to the prepared baking sheet to drain. Place the sheet in the oven while you fry the remaining green tomatoes.

Arrange the fresh tomatoes on 6 to 8 small plates and top with the fried tomato slices. Scatter the small tomatoes over the sliced tomatoes and sprinkle with the crumbled goat cheese and bacon. Top with strips of basil.

Drizzle the balsamic reduction over each plate and top with more basil strips. Serve with additional balsamic reduction, if desired.

Serves 6 to 8.

TIP: I use Roma tomatoes when beefsteak are out of season.

* Bacon grease gives the fried tomatoes a little more flavor, but it burns much more quickly.

A GREAT CREAMY CAESAR SALAD

I have been making this Caesar salad for many years at my house. The recipe is stained with oil from use, and I can't remember where it came from. It is more trouble than buying a bottled dressing, but it is soooo good. Enjoy!

1	large head Romaine lettuce	1	tablespoon lemon juice
7	cloves garlic	1	teaspoon Worcestershire sauce
3/4	cup mayonnaise	1	teaspoon Dijon mustard
4	canned, rolled anchovy fillets with capers*		salt and pepper to taste
1/2	cup grated Parmesan cheese, divided		Gabriel's Garlicky Croutons (page 256)

Remove the end from the Romaine and pull off any brown-tipped leaves. Rinse the lettuce in lots of cold water and set aside to dry.

In the bowl of a food processor mince the garlic. Add the mayonnaise, anchovies with capers, 2 tablespoons Parmesan cheese, lemon juice, Worcestershire sauce, and mustard. Process until the anchovies and capers are thoroughly combined with the other ingredients. Season with salt and pepper and mix lightly. Set aside.

Chop the Romaine into bite-size pieces and place in a large bowl. Toss with enough dressing to coat. Add the remaining 2/3 cup Parmesan cheese and the croutons, tossing to blend. Serve immediately.

Serves 4 to 6.

* If you aren't a fan of anchovies try the Caesar salad without anchovies on page 47.

BEEF AND BARLEY SOUP

My friend Gail Schwartz from Bible study brings the most delicious food when we have our potluck dinners. This was a great soup that we enjoyed with her cheese biscuits (page 237) on a cold winter night in January. So easy but so good!

1 pound skirt or flank steak strips, diced*	3 to 4 carrots, chopped
1 medium onion, chopped	4 to 5 (8-ounce) cans beef bouillon
3 to 4 stalks celery, chopped	1 teaspoon garlic salt
	1/2 to 3/4 cup pearl barley

In a large stockpot add the steak, onion, celery, and carrots. Cover the steak and vegetables with water. Cook uncovered for 15 to 20 minutes.

Add the beef bouillon and garlic salt. Boil another 10 minutes.

Add the pearl barley. Continue to cook, uncovered, until the barley is done, 30 to 45 minutes.

If the soup is too thick after the barley has cooked, add one more can of bouillon.

Serves 6 to 8.

* Get this meal on the table even faster by purchasing the presliced fajita meat at your supermarket.

BLACK-EYED PEA AND HAM SOUP

Joan Glover is one of my Bible study sisters. She brought this to our kickoff dinner for a new study. It went so fast I didn't even get to try it that night. Serve it with the cheese biscuits on page 237 for a truly delicious meal.

4	tablespoons vegetable or olive oil, divided	3	cups beef stock
1	cup diced celery	1	center cut ham slice
1	cup chopped onion	2	teaspoons dried oregano
2	(15-ounce) cans black-eyed peas or 24 ounces frozen black-eyed peas	2	teaspoons Italian seasoning
		1	teaspoon garlic powder
2	(14.5-ounce) cans diced tomatoes	1	teaspoon salt
2	cups water	2	tablespoons honey
		1½	teaspoons sugar

In a large stockpot add 2 tablespoons of oil and sauté the celery and onions until crisp tender. Add the peas, tomatoes, water, and beef stock.

In a medium sauté pan heat 2 tablespoons of oil. Cut the ham into smaller pieces and place in the sauté pan. Cook the ham pieces until cooked through but not browned. Add a couple of tablespoons of water if needed to keep it from getting too brown. Set aside to cool. Place the cooled meat in a food processor and finely chop. Add the chopped meat to the stockpot.

Add the oregano, Italian seasoning, garlic powder, salt, honey, and sugar.

Cook about 1 hour, adding more water if needed.

Makes 12 cups.

CAESAR SALAD WITHOUT ANCHOVIES

Alexis Edwards Amaden has this recipe for Caesar salad for people who don't care for anchovies. I love a Caesar salad with the fresh lemon juice and Parmesan cheese over crisp greens on a hot summer evening. You can put a piece of leftover salmon, steak, grilled chicken, or crab cake on a Caesar and have a delicious meal in no time. I love to be in the kitchen, but not for too long during our Southern summer months.

1 bunch Romaine lettuce	1 egg yolk
1/4 cup extra-virgin olive oil	juice of 1/2 lemon
2 to 3 cloves garlic, minced or pressed	3 tablespoons white vinegar
1/2 cup grated Parmesan cheese	1/4 teaspoon salt

Wash the lettuce and tear it into bite-size pieces.

In a large bowl add the olive oil, garlic, Parmesan cheese, egg yolk, lemon juice, white vinegar, and salt. Stir well. Add the Romaine lettuce and toss. Serve immediately.

Serves 2 to 4.

VARIATION: Leave the Romaine leaves whole and arrange them on the plate for a different presentation. Drizzle the dressing on top of the lettuce when you're ready to serve.

Butternut Squash Soup

Our executive chef at Gabriel's, Brian Charles, counts this as one of his best soups. He often serves this on Saturday, our Chef's Choice soup day. It is good hot or room temperature, topped with a little crème fraiche* and nutmeg or with nutmeg and toasted almonds.

1³/4	pounds butternut squash	1	quart chicken stock
2	tablespoons olive oil	1¹/2	cups milk
3/4	cup rough chopped yellow onion	1¹/2	cups heavy cream
1/3	cup plus 1 tablespoon coarsely chopped celery	1	tablespoon kosher salt
1¹/2	teaspoons fresh garlic	1/3	cup plus 1 tablespoon honey
1/4	teaspoon ground nutmeg	3¹/2	ounces blonde roux**

Peel, seed, and coarsely chop the squash. In a large stockpot, heat the oil and add the onion, celery and squash. Cover and sweat the vegetables over medium heat until the onion and celery are tender. Add the garlic, nutmeg, and stock, and bring the mixture to a simmer, cooking uncovered until the squash is tender. Add the milk, cream, and salt.

Transfer to a blender in batches, and purée until smooth. Return the soup to the stockpot and add the honey and the roux. Bring the soup back up to a simmer for 5 minutes. Serve hot or room temperature.

Makes 2¹/2 quarts.

* To make crème fraiche: combine 1 cup whipping cream and 2 tablespoons buttermilk in a glass container. Cover and let stand at room temperature (about 70°F) from 8 to 24 hours, or until very thick. Stir well before covering, and refrigerate up to 10 days. Because crème fraiche can be boiled without curdling, it is the ideal addition for sauces or soups. It is also delicious spooned over fresh fruit or other desserts, such as warm cobblers or puddings.

** See the glossary for tips on how to get the perfect roux.

CHICKEN AND CORN CHOWDER

This recipe was a staple for Liz Cole's family as she grew up on the Mississippi Gulf coast. It served as a nice alternative to seafood chowder.

4 slices thick-cut bacon, diced	ground cayenne pepper to taste
1 large yellow onion, small dice	nutmeg to taste
2 large stalks celery, small dice	1/2 cup heavy cream
2 cups chicken broth	1/2 cup (firmly packed) fine, soft,
3 cups frozen sweet white corn	white bread crumbs
kernels, thawed	2 cups diced cooked chicken
2 cups whole milk	1/4 cup thinly sliced green onion tops
salt and black pepper to taste	2 tablespoons chopped parsley

In a large saucepan cook the bacon over medium heat until the fat is rendered and the bacon is golden brown. Add the onion and celery, and sauté until translucent and softened but not colored, about 5 minutes. Add the broth and corn. Bring to a simmer and cook, stirring often, until the vegetables are tender, about 10 minutes.

Add the milk and season well with salt, pepper, cayenne, and nutmeg. Bring the mixture back up to a simmer.

Add the cream, bread crumbs, and chicken, and simmer, stirring often, until the crumbs dissolve completely and the chowder is thick, about 10 minutes more. Taste and adjust seasoning. Ladle into heated bowls and sprinkle with green onions and parsley.

Serves 10 to 12.

CORNBREAD SALAD

We serve a cornbread salad at Gabriel's. It is one of our customers' favorite cold salads. It combines some of my favorite things: cornbread, tomatoes, bacon, and mayonnaise.

1	(7-ounce) package cornbread mix, plus ingredients to make cornbread	4	medium tomatoes, peeled and chopped
1	cup mayonnaise	1	green bell pepper, diced
1/4	cup sweet pickle juice	1/2	small onion, chopped
		1/2	cup chopped sweet pickles
		9	slices bacon, cooked and crumbled

Make the cornbread according to the package directions and bake in an 8-inch square pan. Cool, crumble, and set aside.

In a small bowl combine the mayonnaise and pickle juice. Stir well and set aside.

In a medium bowl combine the tomatoes, peppers, onion, sweet pickles, and bacon.

Layer half of the cornbread mixture in a large glass bowl. Top with half of the mayonnaise mixture and then the tomato mixture. Repeat layers with the remaining mixtures. Cover and chill 2 hours before serving. If the mixture is a little dry after you toss it together, add a little more mayonnaise and pickle juice.

Serves 8.

VARIATIONS: Try other vegetables in this salad. Here are some suggestions:
    3/4 cup chopped cauliflower
    3/4 cup chopped broccoli
    3/4 cup chopped carrots
    3/4 cup chopped celery

TIP: Feel free to use leftover cornbread for this recipe.

Frozen Fruit Salad

This is just perfect for that Southern ladies luncheon or for any ladies luncheon, for that matter. Variations of a frozen salad have been around for years, but I love this lower-fat version using the nonfat peach yogurt and low-fat sour cream.

1	(8-ounce) carton nonfat peach yogurt	2	bananas, sliced
1	(8-ounce) carton low-fat sour cream	1	(8¼-ounce) can crushed pineapple, drained
½	cup sugar	¼	cup maraschino cherries
	juice of 1 lemon	¼ to ½	cup chopped pecans
			dash of salt

In a medium bowl mix the yogurt, sour cream, and sugar. Add the lemon juice, bananas, pineapple, cherries, pecans, and salt. Stir well. Pour the mixture into muffin tins lined with aluminum baking cups and freeze. Take them out of the freezer about 45 minutes before serving. They will keep in the freezer for a month.

Makes 18 servings.

NOTE: There are some really decorative baking cups on the market right now. Check them out online for some colorful additions to your table.

HOT SPINACH SALAD

A spinach salad with egg and bacon has been around in many versions for a while now. This one is a little different in that it doesn't use the bacon grease in the dressing. I love spinach just about any way, raw, sautéed, steamed, or creamed. Me and Popeye!

1	clove garlic, peeled and slivered	1/4	teaspoon salt
1/3	cup olive oil		dash of pepper
10 to 12	ounces fresh spinach, washed and dried	2	hard-cooked eggs, chopped
1/4	cup red wine vinegar	4	slices bacon, crisply cooked and crumbled

In a small bowl let the garlic clove stand in the olive oil for 1 hour and then remove.

Place the spinach into a salad serving bowl and refrigerate if not serving right away.

In a small saucepan heat the garlic-infused oil, vinegar, salt, and pepper, stirring occasionally. Toss the hot dressing with the spinach until the leaves are well coated. Sprinkle the chopped eggs and bacon over the salad and toss lightly.

Serves 4.

FRENCH ONION SOUP

Thanks to Liz Cole for reminding me how much I love French onion soup. You'll love it, too, when you see how easy this soup is to prepare.

2	teaspoons olive oil	1/4	teaspoon salt
4	cups thinly sliced Vidalia or other sweet onion	1/4	cup dry white wine
		8	cups low-sodium beef broth
4	cups thinly sliced red onion	1/4	teaspoon chopped fresh thyme
1/2	teaspoon sugar	8	(1-ounce) slices French bread
1/2	teaspoon freshly ground pepper	8	(1-ounce) slices Swiss cheese

Heat the olive oil in a Dutch oven over medium-high heat. Add the onions to the pan and sauté for 5 minutes or until tender. Stir in the sugar, pepper, and salt. Reduce the heat to medium and cook for 20 minutes, stirring frequently.

Increase the heat to medium-high and sauté for 5 minutes or until the onions are golden brown. Stir in the wine and cook for 1 minute. Add the broth and thyme; bring to a boil. Cover, reduce heat, and simmer for 2 hours.

Preheat the broiler.

Place the bread slices in a single layer on a baking sheet; broil for 2 minutes or until toasted, turning after 1 minute. Cut bread into 1-inch cubes.

Place eight ovenproof bowls on a sheet pan. Ladle 1 cup of soup into each bowl. Divide bread cubes evenly among the bowls, and top each bowl with a cheese slice. Broil 3 minutes or until the cheese begins to brown.

Serves 8.

GREEK TOMATO AND PEPPER SALAD

My sister-in-law, Jeri Sandifer, shared this recipe with my daughter Stephanie Bahm. It's now one of her favorites that she makes on special occasions. Stephanie likes a variety of foods and textures and doesn't mind spending time in the kitchen. Both of my grandsons, Wyatt and Heath, have some dishes that they love to make with her. Laney Katherine, my three-year-old granddaughter, wants to join in, but so far she can just make a mess.

1 cup extra-virgin olive oil	1 each green, red, yellow, and orange peppers, cut into 1/2-inch strips
4 tablespoons red wine vinegar	
2 teaspoons salt	
1 teaspoon black pepper	1 red onion, thinly sliced
1 1/2 teaspoons dried thyme	10 ounces feta cheese, coarsely crumbled
1 pound cherry tomatoes, cut in halves or fourths	
	1 cup pitted sliced black olives
	1 head Bibb lettuce

In a large bowl whisk together the olive oil, vinegar, salt, black pepper, and thyme. Add the cherry tomatoes, sliced peppers, red onion, feta cheese, and black olives.

To serve place a whole lettuce leaf on each salad plate, and spoon the tomatoes and peppers over each leaf.

Serves 8.

Vichyssoise
(Leek–Potato Soup)* "Your Way"

Dawn McEachern, wife of chef Tom McEachern, served this dish at her house on New Year's Eve several years ago. Dawn is part of a dinner group of fourteen or so folks who take turns hosting the New Year's Eve dinner. Dawn served this soup with a seafood option with truffle oil, and everyone loved it.

1	pound leeks, cleaned and dark green sections removed (4 to 5 medium)	14	ounces Yukon gold potatoes (4 small), peeled and diced small
3	tablespoons unsalted butter kosher salt, plus additional for seasoning	1	quart vegetable stock or broth
		1	cup heavy cream
		1	cup buttermilk
		1/2	teaspoon white pepper
		1	tablespoon snipped chives

Chop the leeks into small pieces. In a 6-quart saucepan over medium heat, melt the butter. Add the leeks and a heavy pinch of kosher salt and sweat** the leeks for 5 minutes. Decrease the heat to medium-low and cook until the leeks are tender, about 25 minutes, stirring occasionally.

Add the potatoes and the vegetable broth, increase the heat to medium-high, and bring to a boil. Reduce the heat to low, cover, and gently simmer until the potatoes are soft, about 45 minutes.

Turn off the heat and purée the mixture with an immersion blender until smooth, or in batches in a blender. Stir in the heavy cream, buttermilk, and white pepper. Taste and adjust seasoning. Sprinkle with chives. Serve warm immediately or ice bath to room temperature and refrigerate for later. Serve warm or chilled.

Makes 2 1/2 quarts.

VARIATION: Place seared scallops, shrimp, lobster, or crabmeat (or a combination) in individual bowls with fried leeks on top. At the table, pour warm soup around the seafood and drizzle with truffle oil using an eyedropper.

TIP: Be sure to wash the leeks, which can collect soil in between the layers. Chopping the leeks in half and soaking them in water will help.

NOTE: This soup would be a great meatless dinner served with a salad and bread.

---

* Leek and potato is a classic combination that is used in the classic French soup, Vichyssoise. It is incredibly versatile, as it can be served warmed or chilled. This version is warm, but the soup can be very refreshing in the spring and summer served chilled.

** See the glossary for tips on sweating vegetables.

DUCK AND CHICKEN GUMBO

I have never really been as big a fan of duck as my husband, Ed, and many of his friends are. But for his birthday I decided I would make a dinner that he would love. His friend Marshall Dye and I decided to tackle the project of a duck gumbo. We researched existing recipes and decided to combine several and make our own. I made this a day ahead, cooled it, and stored it in the refrigerator overnight. I pulled all the bones out of the gumbo before I reheated it. Real "gumbo folks" tell me that it is even better the day after it is made.

3/4 to 1 cup canola oil, divided
2 (4- to 6-pound) ducks, domestic or wild (mallard, pintails, or teals), skin removed and cut into pieces
1 teaspoon salt
1 teaspoon pepper
1 pound andouille sausage, cut into 1/2-inch slices
1/2 cup all-purpose flour
3 quarts chicken broth, divided
1 cup chopped parsley, divided
1 teaspoon dried thyme
1 1/2 teaspoons dried marjoram
2 bay leaves

1/2 teaspoon dried sage
2 teaspoons Creole seasoning
1 whole roasted chicken, skinned, pulled, and chopped into 1/2-inch pieces
1 1/2 cups frozen yellow corn
2 tomatoes, diced and seeded
1/4 cup olive oil
1 large Vidalia onion, chopped
1 red bell pepper, chopped
2 stalks celery, chopped
3 garlic cloves, minced
1 tablespoon gumbo file*
3 cups cooked wild rice
Hot sauce

Heat a large stockpot over medium heat. Add 1/2 cup of the canola oil and heat until hot. Sprinkle the duck pieces with salt and pepper and add to the pot, cooking and turning the pieces until browned on all sides, 5 to 7 minutes. Remove the pieces and set aside. Pour out the oil and clean the pan with a paper towel.

Heat the same pot over medium-high heat until it is hot. Add the remaining 1/4 cup canola oil and the sausage pieces. Cook, stirring until browned. Remove the sausage pieces and set aside. Turn the heat to low and pour the drippings into a measuring cup, adding more oil to measure 1/2 cup, if needed, and pour it back into the pot.

Place the pot back over the low heat and sprinkle 1/2 cup flour over the oil, whisking to combine. Cook and whisk over very low heat 10 to 12 minutes, or until the flour and oil form a dark roux.** Add 2 to 3 cups of the broth, whisking until the mixture is smooth. Add 3/4 cup of the parsley, the thyme, marjoram, bay leaves, sage, and Creole seasoning, stirring into the liquid to combine. Add the duck, sausage, chicken, corn, tomatoes, and the remaining broth. Bring to a boil and let simmer, stirring occasionally.

Heat a separate skillet over medium heat. Add the olive oil and cook the onion, bell pepper, celery, and garlic just until tender. Drain any remaining oil from the skillet and add the vegetable mixture to the duck mixture. Bring back to a boil, lower the heat, and let simmer 2 to 3 hours. Ten minutes before serving, turn off the heat, add the file, and let stand a few minutes to thicken.

Serve over wild rice. Garnish with the remaining 1/4 cup parsley. Be sure hot sauce is on the table for folks to use.

Serves 8 to 10.

* Gumbo file is a powder made of dried and ground sassafras leaves.

** See "roux" in the glossary.

PEOPLE—
VALUABLE INGREDIENTS
IN MY LIFE

I met Tom McEachern through the Dunaway family, who owned the 1848 House, an antebellum mansion converted into a restaurant. Tom worked as the executive chef.

My husband, Ed, was the contractor for the renovations that began almost as soon as Bill Dunaway purchased the mansion. As you can imagine, the repairs were ongoing in a house of that vintage. Ed supervised the renovations, and Tom taught Ed cooking techniques. After hearing Ed talk about such a talented chef, I wanted to eat there as often as possible. That was my introduction to Tom, who contributed a large number of recipes to *Second Helpings*. Throughout the years I have admired Tom and watched him cook in three different restaurants. He taught in a Florida culinary school and is a James Beard Award winner.

The Dunaways and McEacherns became permanently joined when Dawn, the Dunaways' oldest daughter, married Tom.

The 1848 House closed in 2001 after the 9/11 attack, and Tom became the executive chef at the Horseradish Grill, where many Atlantans enjoyed his gifted touch with beloved Southern dishes. In 2007 he became the executive chef at Ray's on the River, providing Atlantans with a fine-dining experience while watching the Chattahoochee River glide by.

When Tom and Dawn decided to do extensive remodeling on their home, they chose Ed to do the job. A great kitchen, dining room, and library for lots and

Tom and Dawn's kitchen . . . before we arrived!

lots of cookbooks and menu planning were an important part of that renovation.

I told you the story of our friendship with the McEacherns for a purpose. When the photo shoot for *Second Helpings* was under discussion, I knew there were a couple of make-it-or-break-it factors in choosing the location. One prerequisite was good lighting; another was the ability to cook at least some of the dishes on site. We also needed to stay close to my home, as four out of the five crew members were staying with us.

When shooting *Cooking in the South*, I called in favors from many cooking friends. We shot fifty to sixty dishes in four days and camped out a large part of each day in a friend's home where the lighting was good. They couldn't use their kitchen other than to make coffee for four days. Styling dishes were everywhere! It was fun and we made it work, but with everyone's busy lifestyle I didn't want to impose on them again.

Gabriel's kitchen and staff is occupied in every nook and cranny from 6:00 a.m. to 9:00 p.m. Monday through Saturday, so that location and group of "volunteers" was out.

While deliberating where in the world conditions would be perfect for the shoot and who we could possibly impose on for four days, Ed suggested Tom and Dawn's kitchen. The light was great, the kitchen fantastic, and they would understand the passion for the *best* food to get the *best* shot to put in the *best* cookbook ever. I approached Dawn; she and Tom mulled over the idea and graciously responded with a hearty *yes*.

A photo shoot is great fun but loads of work. Attending the shoot for *Second Helpings* were myself; the photographer, Ron Manville; the food stylist, Libbie Summers; my editor from Thomas Nelson, Heather Skelton; and Debbie Willyard, our chef for the shoot, who is also a good friend. A bunch of foodies—talking, living, cooking, and styling food for four straight days. Fun for us—craziness for anyone who wants their days to be normal and balanced.

What a week that was. Once again styling dishes were *everywhere*, garnishes and cheeses and quarts of cream filled the McEachern refrigerator—the dining room table and chairs shoved to one side of the room, pots and pans on the stove and in the ovens, and an endless sink of dirty dishes and pans to be washed, dried, and used again. Sounds like a nightmare unless you live and breathe food. What a project! What a great team we had, ending with a beautiful accomplishment that I hope will bring you and your cooking friends and family enjoyment for many years to come.

Libbie and I decorating cupcakes.

Smoky Chipotle Grilled Baby Back Ribs (page 112)

ENTREES

PORK SCALLOPS
WITH ROSEMARY WINE SAUCE

A Liz Cole "good for company" recipe!

- -

4	(3/4-inch-thick) boneless pork chops (about 1 pound) Salt and pepper to taste	1	tablespoon olive oil
		2	teaspoons minced fresh rosemary or 1 teaspoon dried
3	tablespoons unsalted butter, divided	1/4	cup dry white salt and pepper

- -

Season the pork chops with salt and pepper. Place the chops between sheets of waxed paper and pound with a meat mallet until about 1/8-inch thick.

In a large skillet over high heat, melt 1 tablespoon of the butter with the olive oil. When the butter foams add the pork chops, reduce the heat to medium-high, and sauté about 3 minutes or until browned. Turn, add the rosemary, and cook 2 to 3 minutes longer, or until browned and cooked through. Be careful not to overcook. Transfer the chops to heated platter.

Deglaze the pan with the white wine to begin the sauce, scraping up any browned bits clinging to the pan. Cook until reduced by about half. Add the remaining 2 tablespoons of butter, 1 tablespoon at a time, whisking until emulsified. Pour over the chops and serve hot.

Serves 4.

HYLTON'S PHEASANT OVER RICE

Hylton Dupree, Esq., is known for his wit, kindness, and patience outside the courtroom and his wit and shrewdness in the courtroom. His nickname from law school is "Smoothie," if that tells you anything about his professional success. I'm always happy to spend time at Hylton's table, especially when he serves his pheasant.

1	cup all-purpose flour	1	quart chicken broth
	Salt and pepper to taste	2	(14-ounce) cans cream of
2 to 3	pheasants cut into bite-size		mushroom soup
	pieces*	2	(14-ounce) cans cream of celery
1/3	cup olive oil		soup
2	onions, chopped	2	cups white rice, cooked according
8	stalks celery, chopped		to directions

Preheat the oven to 350 degrees.

Place the flour, salt and pepper, and pheasant in a plastic bag and shake to coat the meat.

Heat a large oven-safe roasting pan on high heat and add the olive oil. When hot, add the pheasant pieces and sear on all sides. Remove the pheasant, lower the heat, and add the onions and celery. Cook until tender.

Add the broth and mushroom and celery soups, and stir to combine. Return the pheasant to the pan and cover. Place in the oven and cook 3 to 4 hours. Serve over rice.

Serves 8.

* If you can't find pheasant, you can substitute quail or chicken.

Red Beans and Rice
with Andouille Sausage

For a twist, try Randy Wynns' Rice Pilaf recipe on page 258.

1	pound dried red kidney beans, washed and picked over, or 3 cans red kidney beans, rinsed		crumbled
		1	teaspoon Tabasco
1 to 2	pounds Andouille sausage*	1/2	teaspoon ground cloves
1	large onion, chopped	1/2	teaspoon freshly ground white pepper
6	cups water if using dried beans (3 cups if using canned beans)	1/2	teaspoon freshly ground black pepper
2	stalks celery with leaves, chopped	1/4	teaspoon cayenne, or to taste
5	cloves garlic, minced	2	teaspoons salt, or to taste
4	bay leaves	2	cups white rice, cooked according to package directions
1	tablespoon dried thyme, crumbled		fresh parsley for garnish
2	teaspoons dried oregano,		

Soak the beans overnight in a bowl with enough water to cover by 2 inches. Drain the beans in a colander and rinse well. Cut the Andouille sausage in half lengthwise. Cut each half into 1/2-inch slices.

In a heavy 6-quart stockpot combine the water, beans, half of the sausage, onion, celery, garlic, bay leaves, thyme, oregano, Tabasco, cloves, white and black pepper, cayenne, and salt. Bring to a boil, cover and simmer for 1 1/2 hours over low heat.

Grill or pan fry the remaining sausage and add to the bean mixture. Barely simmer for 1 hour, adding more water if the mixture becomes too thick.

Cook the rice according to the package directions.

Remove 1 cup of beans and mash with a potato masher. Return to the pot and incorporate well, simmering another 5 minutes.

Place 1/2 to 3/4 cup cooked rice in a bowl and top with beans and sausage. Garnish with chopped fresh parsley.

Serves 6 to 8 as an entrée.

* Use 1 pound of sausage if serving as a side dish and 2 pounds if serving as an entrée.

ROASTED
BUTTERNUT SQUASH LASAGNA

This is another great recipe from Mary Gillis. I think cooking is a creative sport for her, if there is such a thing. Her family and friends will use any excuse to gather for her new creations. Mary served this butternut squash sauce over spaghetti noodles, garnishing it a bit differently by adding some sautéed fresh sage and toasted walnuts and topping it with freshly grated Parmesan cheese. Take a recipe, experiment, and make it your own.

3	pounds butternut squash, peeled, seeded, and diced		crumbled (or 8 tablespoons chopped fresh)
3	tablespoons vegetable oil	1	tablespoon minced garlic
	Salt for seasoning	4	tablespoons flour
1/4	cup plus 1 to 2 tablespoons unsalted butter		Salt and pepper to taste
		9	lasagna noodles, uncooked
1	large onion, diced	3/4	cup freshly grated Parmesan cheese
1	pound sliced portabella mushrooms	3/4	cup grated Gruyère cheese
1	pound ground Italian sausage	1	cup heavy creamy
4	cups milk	1/2	teaspoon salt
2	tablespoons dried rosemary,		Fresh rosemary sprigs for garnish

Preheat the oven to 450 degrees and oil 2 large shallow baking pans.

In a large bowl toss the squash with the oil until coated, and spread in a single layer in the pans. Roast the squash for 10 minutes, stir and season with salt. Roast another 15 minutes or until tender and turning golden.

While the squash is roasting, preheat a skillet at medium heat and add 1 to 2 tablespoons of the butter. Add the onions and sauté. When the onions begin to soften add the mushrooms and cook another 5 minutes. Remove the mixture from the skillet and place in a bowl.

Brown the sausage in the same skillet. Drain the sausage and combine with the mushroom mixture, mixing gently but thoroughly.

In a saucepan bring the milk to a simmer with the rosemary. Heat the milk over low heat for 10 minutes, and strain into a measuring cup.

In a large heavy saucepan heat the remaining 1/4 cup butter and heat over moderately low heat. Add the garlic and stir until softened. Stir in the flour to create a roux. Stir 3 minutes, until the flour is cooked.

Remove the pan from the heat and gradually whisk in the milk. Return the pan to the heat and simmer the sauce for 10 minutes, whisking occasionally. The sauce will get thick. Stir in the squash and salt and pepper to taste.

Reduce the oven heat to 375 degrees and butter a 13 x 9 x 2-inch baking dish.

Pour 1 cup of the sauce into the baking dish (sauce will not cover the bottom of the dish) and cover with 3 lasagna noodles, making sure they don't touch.

Spread 1/2 of the remaining sauce over the pasta, then a layer of 1/2 the sausage mixture. Top the first layer with not quite 1/2 of the Parmesan and Gruyère cheese (leaving some of the cheeses to top the finished dish). Create one more layer, in the same order, and top with the last three lasagna noodles.

In a small bowl beat the heavy cream with the salt until it holds a soft peak. Spread evenly over pasta, making sure pasta is completely covered, sprinkling the remaining Parmesan and Gruyère over the cream. Cover the dish tightly with foil, tenting to keep the foil from touching the cream. Bake in the center of the oven for 30 to 40 minutes. Remove the foil and continue to bake another 10 minutes, or until the top is bubbling and golden. Let stand for 5 minutes before serving.

Garnish each serving with a curl of fresh Parmesan and a sprig of fresh rosemary, if desired.

Serves 12 to 16

VARIATION: For a vegetarian meal leave out the Italian sausage.

FAZZIOS' FRIED SHRIMP ON CHURCH STREET

Jan and Larry Fazzio love to cook, and have fun doing it. "Nobody loves shrimp more than we do," says Larry. "We love shrimp so much we bought our own shrimp boat with a little diesel engine and a 40-foot trawl net. The last time Jan and I had it out on the bay off Carrabelle, Florida, we caught 60 pounds in 2 hours. Good stuff, huh?"

	Canola oil, for frying	1	tablespoon Italian seasoning
1/2	pound (per person) wild-caught shrimp, peeled and deveined	1	teaspoon ground pepper
		1	teaspoon dill weed
1	cup self-rising yellow cornmeal	1	tablespoon fennel seeds
1	cup all-purpose flour	1	lemon

Pour 1 inch of canola oil in a deep pan and turn on high heat. Keep the shrimp in the refrigerator while you prepare the batter. In a medium bowl combine the yellow cornmeal, flour, Italian seasoning, ground pepper, dill weed, and fennel seeds.

Wash the shrimp under cold water and drain. Coat the shrimp in the batter. Drop a little batter in the oil to test it. When the batter sizzles it is ready. Carefully drop the battered shrimp into the hot oil. Lightly stir the shrimp in the oil for 1 to 2 minutes, until they are golden brown.

Place the shrimp on paper towels and squeeze one whole lemon over them while they are still hot. Serve immediately.

Serves 4.

NOTE: Start with wild-caught shrimp that are either fresh or were frozen at sea. Just because the market says they are fresh doesn't mean they just came out of the water. It usually means "never frozen." Truly fresh shrimp have only been out of the water 3 to 5 days, with the heads removed the day they were caught or soon after. And they should have been on ice the whole time.

TIP: Experiment with different herbs and spices for different flavors.

Beef Wellington
with Bearnaise and Merlot Sauce

My friend Mary Gillis has such fun in the kitchen. She makes every recipe her own. Her family and friends love her recipe experiments. For Christmas she made everyone individual Beef Wellingtons. We prepared them together one night when we were discussing recipes for this cookbook, and they were delicious! You've got to make them for your next special occasion.

Pâtè:
- 2 tablespoons unsalted butter
- 4 cloves garlic, minced
- 2 shallots, chopped
- 6 ounces beef, finely chopped
- 2 tablespoons Dijon mustard
- 1 (8-ounce) container button mushrooms, sliced

Merlot sauce:
- 1/4 cup unsalted butter, melted
- 1 clove garlic, chopped
- 1 shallot, diced small
- 1/4 cup all-purpose flour
- 1/2 cup Merlot wine
- 2 cups beef broth
  Salt and pepper to taste

Béarnaise sauce:
- 1/2 cup white wine
- 1 tablespoon finely chopped scallions or shallots
- 1 to 2 teaspoons tarragon
- 3 egg yolks
- 1/2 teaspoon salt
- 1 (4-ounce) stick butter, melted
- 1 teaspoon fresh lemon juice
  Parsley, chopped

Beef Wellingtons:
- 1 (17.3-ounce) package puff pastry sheets
- 8 (6-ounce) beef filet mignons (about 3/4-inch thick), seasoned with black pepper
- 1/4 cup Dijon mustard, divided
- 1/2 cup Gorgonzola cheese, divided
- 2 cups pâtè
- 1 egg, beaten
  Sesame seeds

Make the pâtè: In a heavy 1-quart saucepan over medium-high heat combine the butter, garlic, shallots, and beef. Sauté until the beef is fully cooked, about 5 minutes. Reduce the heat and add the mustard and mushrooms, cooking until the mushrooms are soft, about 5 to 10 minutes.

Using a heavy, wooden spoon, mix and mash all ingredients until the mixture forms a paste-like consistency. Remove from the heat and allow to cool.

Put the mixture in a blender and pulse until it is a spreadable consistency.

Make the Merlot sauce: In a large skillet melt the butter over medium heat. Add the garlic and shallots and sauté 3 to 5 minutes, until they become a light golden color. Remove from the heat, add the flour, and stir until smooth. Return to the stove over low heat. Cook and stir until mixture becomes a medium roux.**

Add the Merlot and beef broth and whisk until all the ingredients are well incorporated. Adjust to medium-high heat and bring the sauce to a boil, stirring constantly until it is reduced by half. Lower the heat and simmer gently. The finished sauce should resemble a brown gravy.

Make the béarnaise sauce: In a small saucepan combine the wine, scallions, and tarragon, cooking until the wine is reduced to a glaze.

In a blender combine the glaze, egg yolks, and salt. Pulse the blender to mix the ingredients.

In the same small saucepan heat the butter until it is bubbling hot. With the blender running, gradually add the hot butter in a steady drizzle until the sauce thickens. Remove from the blender and fold in the lemon juice, chopped parsley, and more tarragon, if desired.

The sauce can be kept warm in the top of a double boiler over barely simmering water while you prepare the Beef Wellingtons.

Make the Beef Wellingtons: Set the puff pastry sheets out to thaw 40 minutes before using.

Pat the filets with paper towels to remove the excess moisture.

Unfold the pastry sheets on a lightly floured surface. With a rolling pin, roll the pastry sheet into two 14-inch squares. Trim 1 inch from all four edges to make 13-inch squares. Cut each square into 4 squares each. You should have 8 squares.

Spread 1 teaspoon of the mustard over the center of each pastry square. Place 1 tablespoon of the Gorgonzola on top of the mustard. Evenly divide the pâte among the 8 pastry squares, mounding slightly, and then place a tenderloin on top.

Fold the 2 opposite pastry corners over the beef, overlapping slightly, and press to seal. Flip the Wellington package over and place on a parchment-lined baking sheet, seam side down. Refrigerate for 1 hour.

Preheat the oven to 425 degrees.

When ready to cook brush the top of the Wellingtons with the beaten egg and sprinkle with sesame seeds. Bake for 20 minutes, until the pastry is golden and a meat thermometer registers 117 degrees* (medium rare) when inserted into the center of the meat.

While the meat is cooking prepare 8 serving plates by ladling a small amount of Merlot sauce onto each plate.

Remove the Wellingtons from the oven and place in the Merlot sauce. Ladle the béarnaise sauce over the Wellingtons and serve immediately. Serve extra sauce on the side.

Serves 8.

NOTE: We used a whole tenderloin and cut our own filets, using the tail trimmings for the pâtè.

TIP: You can prepare the pâtè and Merlot sauce ahead of time, but the béarnaise sauce should be prepared just before using.

---

* If you would like your meat more done, decrease the thickness of the filet.

** See the glossary for helpful hints on making the perfect roux.

Beef Tenderloin à la Randy Webb

The Webbs love to tailgate at the University of Georgia football games. Randy and Pam set up their own grill and serve this tenderloin. I'll bet there are a lot of hungry Dawgs hanging around their table. Try it with their favorite Herb Tenderloin Sauce (page 252).

4 to 6 pounds trimmed whole beef
    tenderloin, small end removed
2 tablespoons kosher salt

Olive oil or teriyaki sauce
Salt and freshly cracked pepper
    to taste

Clean the tenderloin and pat dry with paper towels. Sprinkle salt evenly on all sides. Place on a rack over a cookie sheet. Refrigerate uncovered for 10 to 12 hours or overnight, up to 24 hours. When ready to cook, bring the beef to room temperature and spread either olive oil or teriyaki sauce over the meat, and season with salt and pepper to your liking.

Preheat the oven to 350 degrees and prepare the grill.

Whether on a charcoal or gas grill, sear the tenderloin on high heat for approximately 15 minutes, turning and searing to get the "bark" or crust that you desire. Rest the meat for 20 to 30 minutes on a greased cookie sheet. Finish cooking the roast in the preheated oven for 15 to 25 minutes. Remove the meat from the oven when a meat thermometer reads 128 degrees.

Rest the meat for 10 to 20 minutes before slicing. Serve with your favorite sauce.

Serves 12 to 20 (4-ounce) portions.

NOTE FROM RANDY: The air brining and resting of the meat during the cooking process make for the most consistently cooked and moist tenderloin I have ever had.

SCALLOPS OVER CHAMPAGNE RISOTTO

Ed took this recipe and adapted it to what has become one of my favorites. Make any day a special occasion with this dish. The rest of that champagne won't hold until the next time you make this dish, so go ahead and enjoy it!

3	tablespoons butter	2	(14¹/₂-ounce) cans low-sodium
1	pound scallops		chicken broth, more if desired
¹/₂	cup chopped shallots	¹/₂	cup grated Reggiano cheese
1¹/₃	cups basmati rice		Salt and pepper to taste
2	cups dry champagne	¹/₄	cup fresh parsley, chopped
		¹/₄	cup almond slices, toasted

In a heavy medium saucepan melt the butter over medium heat. Once the pan is hot add the scallops and sear on both sides for 1 minute. Remove the scallops and set aside. In the same pan add the shallots and sauté for 1 minute. Add the rice and sauté for 1 minute. Add the champagne and simmer, stirring often, until almost all of the liquid evaporates, about 2 to 3 minutes. Add the broth and simmer, stirring often, until the rice is almost tender, about 15 minutes.

Add the scallops back to the pan and simmer until they are cooked through and the rice is tender, about 5 minutes, stirring often. The mixture should be creamy. Add more broth if it becomes too thick. Stir in the Reggiano and season with salt and pepper.

To serve, top with chopped parsley and almonds.

Serves 4.

CHICKEN FRANCAISE

Another good and quick dinner option from Liz Cole. Also nice enough for company!

1/4	cup white wine	2	whole boneless, skinless chicken
1/2	cup chicken broth		breasts (pounded flat)
1	tablespoon fresh lemon juice	1	ounce sun-dried tomatoes,
1/8	teaspoon salt		chopped
1/4	teaspoon white pepper	4	ounces fresh spinach
1	teaspoon garlic, minced		Linguine or your favorite pasta,
2	ounces olive oil		cooked according to package
1	cup all-purpose flour		directions
2	eggs, beaten		

In a medium bowl combine the wine, chicken broth, lemon juice, salt, pepper, and garlic and set aside.

In a 12-inch pan add the oil and preheat on medium-high heat.

Place the flour in shallow pan. In another shallow pan place the beaten eggs. Dredge the chicken breasts first in flour and then in the eggs. Once the oil is hot, place the chicken breasts in the pan and sauté on both sides until lightly brown.

Leaving the chicken in the pan, discard half of the oil from the pan. Add a pinch of flour to the remaining oil and chicken. Add the wine mixture and simmer until the liquid has reduced by half.

Add the sun-dried tomatoes and fresh spinach and cook just until the spinach has wilted.

Serve over linguine or your favorite pasta.

Serves 4.

CHICKEN SALAD CASSEROLE

My friend Trish Elliott is known for this chicken casserole in and outside of the large Elliott family. Trish is always asked to make this for wedding or baby showers, especially if it is a ladies-only party.

4	cups cubed cooked chicken		1 1/2	cups slivered almonds, divided
2	cups diced celery		1/4	cup fresh lemon juice
1 1/2	cups stuffing mix, divided		1	tablespoon grated onion
2	cups Miracle Whip*		1 1/2	cups grated cheese, divided
1/2	cup chicken stock			

Preheat the oven to 350 degrees.

In a large bowl, mix together the chicken, celery, 1 cup of the stuffing mix, Miracle Whip, chicken stock, 1 cup of the almonds, lemon juice, onion, and 1 cup of the cheese and spread into a 9 x 13-inch casserole dish.

In a medium bowl mix the remaining 1/2 cup stuffing mix, the remaining 1/2 cup almonds, and the remaining 1/2 cup grated cheese and spread over the chicken mixture.

Bake for 30 minutes.

Serves 10 to 12.

* Use Miracle Whip instead of mayonnaise so you can make this recipe ahead of time and freeze it.

COPPER RIVER SALMON CAKES

Executive Chef Tom McEachern serves this dish at Ray's on the River when the Copper River Salmon are in season, from mid–May to mid–June. If salmon aren't in season, you can find wild–caught salmon at your local grocery store.

1	quart saltine crackers (2³/4 sleeves)	1/4	cup parsley, chopped
1	egg	1	jalapeño, seeded and minced
2	egg yolks	1¹/4	cups mayonnaise
1	teaspoon garlic powder	3/4	cup red bell pepper, roasted,
1¹/2	teaspoons dry mustard		peeled, seeded, and diced
1/2	teaspoon celery seeds	2	pounds Copper River King
1¹/4	teaspoons salt		salmon, diced small
1/4	teaspoon black pepper	1	cup Ritz crackers, crumbled
1	tablespoon lemon juice		Panko bread crumbs
6	scallions, white part only, minced		Vegetable oil

In a food processor, coarsely chop the crackers.

In a large bowl combine the egg, egg yolks, garlic powder, dry mustard, celery seeds, salt, pepper, lemon juice, scallions, parsley, jalapeños, mayonnaise, and bell peppers. Add the saltine crackers to the vegetable mixture. Carefully fold in the salmon. Fold in the Ritz crackers.

Place the Panko crumbs in a shallow dish. Scoop the salmon mixture into 2- or 4-ounce patties and roll in the Panko crumbs. Preheat a skillet with vegetable oil and sauté the salmon patties until golden brown. Turn and brown on other side.

Makes 20 (2-ounce) cakes or 10 (4-ounce) cakes.

NOTE: Serve topped with Salsa Cruda (page 249).

CROWN PORK ROAST WITH MAPLE, CRANBERRY, PEACH BRANDY SAUCE

Ed and I cooked this for a show at the Strand Theater on the Square in Marietta. What fun we had, and the food was delicious! The peach flavor is a great addition.

Rub:
- 2 (5- to 5¹/2-pound) crown pork roasts
- 2 tablespoons sugar
- 2 tablespoons smoked paprika
- 1 tablespoon plus 1 teaspoon seasoning salt
- 1 tablespoon plus 1 teaspoon dry mustard
- 1 tablespoon plus 1 teaspoon sea salt
- 1 tablespoon plus 1 teaspoon celery salt
- 1 tablespoon plus 1 teaspoon garlic salt
- 1 tablespoon black pepper
- 2 teaspoons onion powder
- 2 teaspoons chili powder
  Cotton twine
  Nonstick cooking spray

Stuffing:
- 9 tablespoons butter
- 1¹/4 cups chopped onion
- 3 cups uncooked instant quick cooking rice
- ¹/2 teaspoon rub mixture
- 3³/4 cups chicken stock
- 1 cup chopped dried peaches
- 1 cup chopped dried cranberries

Sauce:
- ³/4 cup jellied cranberry sauce
- ¹/2 cup maple syrup
- 2 tablespoons Dijon mustard
- 1¹/2 teaspoons grated orange peel
- ¹/4 teaspoon sea salt
- ¹/8 teaspoon black pepper
- ¹/2 cup peach brandy

Prepare the pork: Wipe the meat dry with a paper towel. With a boning knife clean the bones of meat* down to the main part of the chop. Retain the meat to put in the bottom of the roasting pan. Make a small cut in between the ribs if necessary to allow you to easily pull the roasts into a circle.

In a small bowl mix the sugar, smoked paprika, seasoning salt, dry mustard, sea salt, celery salt, garlic salt, black pepper, onion powder, and chili powder. Generously coat both sides of the roast with the rub. Stand the ribs upright and bring the ends to meet to form a circle. Wrap cotton twine several times around the roast and tie off the ends to hold the crown shape. If you're doing this by yourself, use long skewers to hold the shape while you're tying the string. Place in a roasting pan that has been sprayed with nonstick cooking spray. Scatter the reserved meat cuttings around the sides of the roast. Set aside and allow the pork to come to room temperature.

Preheat the oven to 350 degrees. Cover the tips of the pork bones with foil and place on the bottom rack of the oven. Roast the pork until an instant read thermometer registers 150 degrees, approximately 3^{1}/$_{2}$ hours.**

When the internal temperature registers 150 degrees, remove the roasts from the oven and tent with aluminum foil, allowing the meat to rest for 20 to 30 minutes before carving.

Prepare the stuffing: In a large saucepan melt the butter over medium heat. Add the chopped onion and cook until tender but not browned. Add the rice, rub mixture, and chicken stock. Bring mixture to a boil, remove from the heat and add the chopped peaches and cranberries. Cover and let stand for 10 minutes.

Prepare the sauce: In a small saucepan add the cranberry sauce, maple syrup, Dijon mustard, grated orange peel, sea salt, and black pepper. Whisk, bringing to a boil over medium heat until smooth and well combined. Add the peach brandy. Stand back from the pan and carefully ignite the brandy. Remove the sauce from the heat and allow to cool.

To serve: Place the roast on a cutting board and remove the foil and strings from the roast. Slice the meat between the bones. Serve each chop with stuffing and warm sauce.

Serves 12.

SERVING TIP: For a great presentation place the meat on a serving tray and pile the rice mixture high in the crown of the meat. Place little white caps on the ribs, if desired, and remove the string. Carve at the table and serve with warmed sauce.

---

* Cleaning the meat from the bone is called "Frenching." Some butchers will do this for you if you ask them.

** Allow 15 to 20 minutes per pound.

Evelyn's Fried Chicken

Evelyn Elliott is the matriarch of the Elliott family. For 30 years or more, my family and many others have enjoyed the Elliott's hospitality at their family's farm in Stroud, Georgia. I think a perfect getaway is sitting in a rocker on the porch at the farm on a clear, spring weekend, when all the trees are greening with their new spring leaves, while anticipating Evelyn's fried chicken and homemade biscuits for dinner.

1   whole fryer cut into pieces plus more legs and breasts (depending on your family's preference)
1   quart buttermilk
3 to 4 cups self-rising flour

48   ounces (more or less) corn oil for frying
Salt and pepper
1   large cast-iron skillet or Dutch oven

Rinse the chicken under hot running water and pat dry with paper towels.* Put the chicken pieces in a large bowl and pour enough buttermilk over them to almost cover. Allow the chicken to sit overnight in the refrigerator if possible, but at least 3 hours.

Into another large bowl, pour 3 or 4 cups of flour. Cover a sheet pan with a couple of layers of paper towels.

In a large skillet pour the corn oil 2½ to 3 inches deep. Heat the oil over medium to medium-high heat until the temperature reaches 375 degrees. The oil is hot enough if it sizzles when you drop a small amount of flour into it.

Working one piece at a time, starting with the dark meat, take a piece of chicken out of the buttermilk, shake off the excess, salt and pepper both sides of the piece, and then dredge the piece in the flour. Shake off the excess and carefully slip the piece into the hot oil.** Continue with chicken pieces until the pan is full but not crowded. Breast pieces should be added skin side down. Adding the chicken pieces will drop the temperature of the oil to about 325 degrees.

After 3 to 4 minutes lift each chicken piece with tongs or a cooking fork to ensure it is browning evenly. If not, adjust its position in the pan a bit and turn the heat down to medium. Continue to cook for 10 to 12 minutes. Turn the chicken over and continue to fry to a golden brown color, another 10 to 12 minutes, adjusting the heat as needed to keep the chicken from browning too fast.

Total cooking time should be 20 to 30 minutes, depending on the size of your chicken pieces. When chicken is golden brown on both sides, pierce a piece to check for doneness. If the juices run clear, it's done. Remove pieces to the paper towel–lined sheet pan and allow to drain a few minutes. Move to a wire rack to cool. Serve hot or at room temperature.

Serves 4.

NOTE: One whole chicken should serve 4 people, I usually estimate $1^{1}/_{2}$ pieces of chicken per person.

ALTERNATE COOKING TIP: Try it with a teaspoon of garlic powder and a little cayenne pepper in the flour mixture.

NOTE: To cover or not to cover? My mother always covered the chicken after it began to brown on each side, but Evelyn keeps hers uncovered for the entire cooking time. Try it both ways and see which way your family likes it. As with any dish, the more times you fry chicken, the more comfortable you will get and the more it will become your dish. And just remember that in the South, if you can fry good chicken, you're always invited to the party!

* Make sure you wash your sink and anything else that raw chicken touches, including your hands, with hot water and soap.

** According to Evelyn's sister, Aunt Kat, you should bread the chicken just before it goes into the oil. She says that letting it sit with breading on it, changes the texture of the crust.

MEDITERRANEAN SHRIMP

Liz Cole is a friend from my Sunday school class and Bible study, but we share many more interests than just our love of the Lord. We both enjoy preparing good food and entertaining friends in our homes. Liz loves to serve this recipe to her guests.

1	pound lemon-pepper linguine (or plain)	4	cloves garlic, crushed
1 1/2	pounds raw shrimp, peeled and deveined	1/2	teaspoon salt
		1/2	teaspoon pepper
2	large tomatoes, coarsely chopped	1/4	teaspoon oregano
1/4	cup olive oil	3/4	cup crumbled feta cheese

Preheat the oven to 425 degrees.

Bring a large pot of water to a boil. Add the linguine to boiling water and cook according to the package directions.

In a large baking dish, combine the shrimp, tomatoes and their juice, olive oil, garlic, salt, pepper, oregano, and feta cheese. The mixture should make a shallow layer in the pan. Bake for 8 minutes. Remove from the oven and stir. Return the mixture to the oven and cook for an additional 3 to 5 minutes, or until the shrimp are just cooked through.

Serve the shrimp mixture over the drained pasta.

Serves 6.

BLUE CHEESE—STUFFED PORK CHOPS

Liz Cole has so many good recipes in her culinary arsenal. I'm so grateful that she's sharing them with me . . . and you.

1/2	cup crumbled blue cheese		1/2	teaspoon chicken granules
2	green onions, thinly sliced		1/8	teaspoon pepper
4	(1-inch thick) bone-in pork loin		3/4	cup milk
	chops, trimmed			crumbled blue cheese (optional)
1	tablespoon all-purpose flour			cracked pepper (optional)
1/4	cup sour cream			

Preheat an outdoor grill to medium-high (350 to 400 degrees).

In a small bowl toss together the crumbled blue cheese and green onions. Cut a 1- to 2-inch horizontal pocket in the chop, 1 inch deep. Divide the blue cheese mixture into 4 portions and stuff the mixture into the pockets, securing the opening on each chop with wooden picks that have been soaked in water for 10 minutes.*

Place the chops on the grill and put the lid down. Grill for 8 minutes on each side, or until done. Remove the wooden picks. Set the chops aside and keep warm.

In a small saucepan combine the flour, sour cream, chicken granules, and pepper. Whisk until smooth. Gradually whisk in the milk. Bring to a boil over medium heat, stirring constantly. Reduce the heat and simmer 3 minutes, continuing to whisk until the mixture is thick and bubbly.

Serve the chops with the sauce. Top with crumbled blue cheese and cracked pepper, if desired.

Serves 4.

---

* This keeps the picks from burning during the grilling process.

GLYNDA'S MESQUITE ROASTED SALMON

If you attend a cocktail party in the West Cobb area of Marietta, Georgia, chances are you will have the opportunity to eat some of Glynda Chalfant's salmon. Seize the chance! I can't tell you how many times I have discovered it on the table at a party, and I am always glad the hosts chose to use her recipe. It's so easy and sooooo good!

1	(2- to 3-pound) whole salmon fillet	2 to 3	stalks celery, coarsely chopped
1	package McCormick Grill Mates Mesquite Marinade	1	(3½-ounce) jar capers, drained
1	large onion, sliced	3 to 4	eggs, boiled and chopped
			Remoulade sauce (page 245)
			Crackers, crostini, or lavash

Rinse the salmon and pat dry with paper towels. In a small bowl prepare the marinade according to the package directions. Place a large sheet of aluminum foil on a baking sheet and lay the fish on the foil. Pour the marinade over the salmon. Fold the foil to seal the salmon. Allow the salmon to marinate at least 15 minutes, or up to 3 hours prior to cooking. Refrigerate if not baking within 20 minutes.

Preheat the oven to 350 degrees. Fold the foil back and place slices of onion and celery over the salmon. Bake for 20 minutes.

Remove from the oven and allow the salmon to rest. When the salmon is room temperature,* carefully place on a serving plate and garnish with capers, chopped egg, the Remoulade sauce, and your choice of crackers, crostini, or lavash. Refrigerate any leftovers.

Serves 10 to 12 on a cocktail buffet.

---

* The salmon is best when served at room temperature. If you have to cook it well ahead of your serving time, refrigerate it and then bring it up to room temperature before serving.

HAM AND CHEESE PIE

Evelyn Elliott made this for her family when she had leftover ham. One of the many frugal habits of her generation is to never throw good food away or let it go to waste in the refrigerator. My mother made lots of vegetable soup with leftover ham. I'll bet Evelyn does too.

2	eggs	1½	cups Swiss cheese, grated
½	cup milk	1½	cups cheddar cheese, grated
½	cup mayonnaise	⅓	cup chopped green onions
1	tablespoon cornstarch		Pepper to taste
1½	cups ham, already cooked and chopped	1	(9-inch) deep dish pie crust, purchased or homemade

Preheat the oven to 375 degrees.

In a large bowl whisk the eggs, milk, and mayonnaise. Whisk in the cornstarch. Add the ham, cheeses, onions, and pepper. Pour into the unbaked pie crust.

Bake 50 to 60 minutes until the center is set and the crust is golden brown. Check after 40 minutes to see if the crust is browning too much. You may need to cover the crust with foil to prevent burning. The pie is done when a sharp knife inserted near the center comes out almost dry. Let sit 10 minutes before serving.

Serves 8.

MARCELLE'S CHICKEN POT PIE

Marcelle and Bill David are two of Marietta's finest cooks. They take pride in serving well-prepared food. From simple fare like this chicken pot pie to more labor intensive gourmet food, all of it is delicious!

1	whole broiler-fryer chicken, cooked and deboned*	1³/4	cups chicken stock
1	(4-ounce) stick butter	1	(14-ounce) can peas and carrots, drained
6	tablespoons flour	2	cups biscuit baking mix, plus ingredients to make biscuits
1	teaspoon Morton's Nature's Season seasoning blend		
1/2	pint whipping cream		

Chop the chicken into bite-size pieces and set aside while you prepare the sauce.

Melt the butter and add the flour to make a white roux.** Keep the heat on low and stir as you cook the flour, so that it doesn't brown. Add the seasoning blend and the whipping cream, stirring and cooking until thickened. Add the chicken stock and continue cooking until the sauce coats the back of a spoon, stirring continuously so the sauce will not scorch. Add the peas and carrots and the chicken.

Pour the pot pie filling into a 2¹/2- to 3-quart baking dish. If preparing ahead, let the mixture cool before topping with biscuits.

Preheat the oven to 400 degrees.

Prepare the biscuits according to package directions. Roll the dough out and cut the biscuits. Place the biscuits, side by side all over the top of the filling. There will be filling showing around the biscuits and the filling will bubble up around the biscuits as they cook. Bake for 20 to 30 minutes, until biscuits are golden brown.

Serves 6.

TIP: If you're in a hurry use defrosted frozen buttermilk biscuits or canned biscuits.

* Marcelle cooks her chicken in a covered roasting pan in the oven. She partially submerges the chicken in water and then adds fresh celery leaves, onion, and parsley, resulting in a rich stock for her roux. If you braise or boil your own chicken, don't throw the stock out. Strain it through a fine mesh sieve or a piece of cheesecloth. If you have extra, pour it into ice cube molds and freeze for another dish.

** See the glossary for tips to make a great roux.

RANDY'S CHURCH CHICKEN

This is a great dish whether you're cooking for a crowd or for a few. Dr. Randy Webb has delivered hundreds of babies in Marietta, Georgia. Maybe thousands! Evidently he delivers when he cooks for his church too. They keep requesting this tasty chicken.

2	cups pineapple juice	1/4	cup red wine vinegar
5	ounces sherry		Pinch of garlic salt
1/2	cup sugar	6 to 8	boneless, skinless chicken
1/2	cup soy sauce		breasts

In a medium bowl combine the pineapple juice, sherry, sugar, soy sauce, red wine vinegar, and garlic salt and mix well until the sugar is dissolved. Set 1/2 cup of marinade aside for basting. Add the chicken to a zip-top bag and pour the remaining marinade over it. Seal the bag and place in the refrigerator to marinate overnight.

Preheat your grill to medium-high and cook the chicken over direct heat for 12 to 15 minutes, basting 2 to 3 times, until chicken is done.

Drizzle the remaining marinade over chicken. Serve whole breasts or slice into long strips.

Serves 6 to 8.

NOTE: The chicken can be prepared ahead of time and kept warm in aluminum foil in the oven until ready to serve.

PICADILLO

Marcelle David is a true culinarian who cooks a variety of dishes for her Southern family to enjoy. This is her rendition of picadillo, a Latin American dish served with rice and black beans.

1/4	cup olive oil		1/4	cup dry red wine
2	pounds ground beef		3	tablespoons tomato sauce
1	medium onion, finely chopped		1	tablespoon wine vinegar
1	large tomato, peeled, seeded, and finely chopped		1/2	teaspoon firmly packed brown sugar
1/2	cup raisins		2 to 3	drops hot pepper sauce
1/2	medium-size green bell pepper, finely chopped			Pinch of freshly grated nutmeg
1	large garlic clove, minced		1/4	cup water
1/2	teaspoon dried oregano, crushed			Salt (optional)
1	bay leaf			Cooked rice
8	pimiento-stuffed olives, thinly sliced		18	pimiento slices

Preheat a large, deep skillet over medium heat. Add the olive oil and beef and cook until browned. Drain about 1/2 of the grease and stir in the onion, tomato, raisins, green pepper, garlic, oregano, and bay leaf. Cover and cook 10 minutes.

Add the olives, wine, tomato sauce, vinegar, brown sugar, hot sauce, and nutmeg. Cook uncovered for 5 minutes.

Stir in the water. Reduce heat to low, cover and simmer for 30 minutes. If liquid is not absorbed, remove cover and continue to cook until water is nearly evaporated. Add salt if necessary.

Serve over rice. Garnish each serving with 3 pimiento slices.

Serves 6.

TIP: Serve with black beans, sautéed banana slices, toasted French bread, and a salad.

SAUTÉED TILAPIA WITH LEMON-PEPPERCORN SAUCE

Meredith Webb Dykes is another great Marietta cook. If you're looking for an easy fish dish to make for your family during a busy week, you're going to love this. For a weekend treat serve with roasted red potatoes with rosemary and fresh asparagus with feta cheese.

3/4	cup chicken broth	1/2	cup all-purpose flour
1/4	cup fresh lemon juice	2	(6-ounce) tilapia fillets
1 1/2	teaspoons drained brine-packed green peppercorns, crushed lightly*		Salt and pepper to taste
		1/4	teaspoon salt
		1/4	cup flour
3	teaspoons butter, divided		Lemon wedges, if desired
1	teaspoon vegetable oil		

In a small bowl mix the broth, lemon juice, and crushed peppercorns. Set aside.

In a large skillet melt 1 teaspoon of the butter with the oil over low heat.

Add the flour to a shallow plate or bowl. Sprinkle the fish with salt and pepper and dredge in flour.

Increase the heat to medium-high until the butter sizzles. Add the fillets and sauté 3 minutes on each side or until fish flakes easily when tested with a fork. Remove from the pan and keep warm.

Add the broth mixture to the pan, scraping to loosen the browned bits. Bring to a boil and reduce to 1/2 cup. Remove from the heat and whisk in the remaining 2 teaspoons butter. Pour the butter over the fillets. Serve with lemon wedges, if desired.

Serves 2.

* If you can't find the brined peppercorns, use plain black peppercorns.

SALMON WITH PISTACHIO CRUNCH

Mary Gillis has been playing in the kitchen again. She took a really good fish and improved on it. Pistachios give a great crunch to this recipe.

4	(6-ounce) salmon fillets*		3	tablespoons honey
1/8	teaspoon salt		1/2	cup soft bread crumbs
1/8	teaspoon pepper		1/2	cup chopped pistachios
4	tablespoons Dijon mustard		1/4	teaspoon chopped parsley
4	tablespoons butter or margarine, room temperature		1 to 2	lemons

Preheat the oven to 350 degrees.

Sprinkle salmon with salt and pepper.

In a small bowl combine the mustard, butter, and honey. Brush on the fillets.

In another small bowl combine the bread crumbs, pistachios, and parsley.

Roll fillets in the crumb mixture and place in a 13 x 9-inch baking dish. Squeeze the juice of 1/2 a lemon over the fillets and bake for 20 to 22 minutes until fish flakes easily. Use extra lemon slices for garnish.

Serves 6.

* Any firm-flesh fish, such as grouper or amberjack, will work with this recipe also.

SAUSAGE AND MUSHROOM PASTA

Here's another recipe from friend and chef Debbie Willyard. Her mother made this dish for the family for years, and Debbie tweaked it a bit. It's flavorful, fast, and good for a crowd.

7	links sweet Italian sausage	1	teaspoon salt
1/2	cup unsalted butter	1	teaspoon dried basil (1 tablespoon fresh)
4	cloves fresh garlic		
3/4 to 1 pound white button mushrooms (or baby bellas)		1	(16-ounce) box spaghetti, prepared according to package directions
2 1/2 to 3 cups half-and-half			
1	tablespoon all-purpose flour	1/4	cup grated Parmesan cheese

In a large sauté pan brown the sausage. Discard the grease and wipe out the pan. When the sausages are cool enough to handle, slice diagonally into bite-size pieces and set aside. In the clean pan melt the butter and sauté the garlic and mushrooms.

In a medium bowl whisk together the half-and-half, flour, salt, and dried basil (if using fresh basil wait to add with the Parmesan cheese). Add the meat and half-and-half mixture to the pan, simmering for 10 minutes until the sauce thickens.

Add the cooked pasta to the sauce, and stir to coat. Add the Parmesan cheese, mix well, and serve immediately.

Serves 4.

SHRIMP
IN A WHITE WINE CREAM SAUCE

Randy Wynns, a past executive chef at Gabriel's, featured this as one of our nightly specials. Simple and delicious!

1	pound 26/30 shrimp, peeled and deveined	1/2	cup heavy cream
1	tablespoon chopped garlic	1/2	pound cold butter
1	cup white wine		Salt and pepper to taste

In a large pan add the shrimp and garlic and sauté briefly.

Remove from the pan and set aside while you prepare the sauce. In the same pan add the white wine and reduce by half. Add the cream and reduce by half. Finish the sauce with cold butter. Toss the shrimp and garlic in the sauce, and salt and pepper to taste.

Serve over rice pilaf. (See recipe on page 258.)

Serves 3 to 4.

SHRIMP CREOLE

This recipe from Dr. Randy Webb was published last year in our local newspaper, the **Marietta Daily Journal.** *In all these years of seeing Randy, I had not known what an accomplished cook he is. He was happy to allow us to publish this for all to see. Enjoy!*

6	slices bacon	6	ounces water
1¹/2	tablespoons all-purpose flour	1	teaspoon salt
1¹/2	cups chopped onion	1	teaspoon black pepper
4	green onions, divided into green and white parts	¹/4	teaspoon cayenne pepper
		2	pounds cooked and peeled shrimp
³/4	cup bell pepper, chopped	3	tablespoons chopped fresh parsley
¹/2	cup celery, chopped		White rice, prepared according to package directions
2 to 3	cloves garlic, minced		
1	(29-ounce) can tomato sauce		

In a large saucepan cook the bacon over medium heat until crispy. Set aside to drain. Discard all but 3 tablespoons of the grease.

Return the pan to the stovetop and stir in the flour over low heat to make a thin roux, 3 to 5 minutes. Add the onion, the white part of the green onions, bell pepper, celery, and garlic, and sauté for 3 to 4 minutes or until softened. The mixture should be dry.

Add the tomato sauce, water, salt, black pepper, and cayenne pepper and simmer over low to medium heat for 25 minutes. Add the shrimp, parsley, crumbled bacon, and green onion tops to the sauce and continue cooking for 10 minutes. Serve over rice.

Serve with a salad and crusty French bread for a simple but delicious meal.

Serves 4 to 6.

SHRIMP DAUPHINE

This is my friend Liz Cole's recipe. Liz is a great cook and loves to entertain. This is a dish she often serves to her guests.

1/4	cup plus 1 to 2 tablespoons unsalted butter, if needed		Fresh ground black pepper to taste
1	pound peeled and deveined 26/30 shrimp, uncooked		Red cayenne pepper to taste
1/2	pound mushrooms (white or baby bellas)	1/8	teaspoon onion powder
1	(8-ounce) bottle clam juice	1/8	teaspoon garlic powder
1	cup heavy whipping cream	1 1/2	tablespoons minced parsley
	Salt to taste	3	green onions, chopped
			Frozen puff-pastry shells, cooked according to package directions
			Curly parsley sprigs, for garnish

In a heavy 10-inch skillet add the ¼ cup butter and melt over medium heat. Turn the heat to medium-high. Add the shrimp and sauté, stirring until the shrimp turn pink, and being careful not to overcook. Since the shrimp are going to be returned to the sauce to heat through, you can almost undercook them at this point. Remove the shrimp with a slotted spoon and set aside.

Add the mushrooms to the skillet* and sauté until liquid is reduced to a glaze and the mushrooms are caramelized. Add the clam juice to deglaze the pan, scraping up all the browned bits from the pan. Cook over medium heat until liquid is reduced by half.

Add the cream, salt, black pepper, cayenne pepper, onion powder, garlic powder, and minced parsley. Reduce by half. Stir in the green onions and return the shrimp to the pan. Cook until the shrimp are heated through.

Serve in baked pastry shells. Garnish with curly parsley.

Serves 6 to 8.

NOTE: Any leftover shrimp can be served over yellow rice or pasta. For a healthier option, use brown rice.

* If the skillet is dry add 1 tablespoon of butter to sauté the mushrooms.

Tom McEachern's Spaghetti and Meatballs

I love spaghetti and meatballs. When Tom told me he had a great recipe, I could hardly believe he even ate such a plebeian dish. This is not a common dish of oregano-filled, heavy sauce, but it's not labor intensive either. It's almost sweet, but with a touch of heat. You'll have to make them to understand.

Meatballs:
- 3 large eggs
- 1 1/2 cups heavy cream
- 1 tablespoon kosher salt
- 1/2 tablespoon black pepper
- 2 pounds ground chuck
- 1 tablespoon parsley, chopped
- 1/2 cup shallots, minced
- 1 cup Progresso bread crumbs

Tomato sauce:
- 1/2 cup extra-virgin olive oil
- 1 Spanish onion, diced
- 8 cloves garlic, peeled and thinly sliced

- 1 teaspoon dried oregano
- 1 1/2 cups peeled, grated, and finely chopped carrot
- 2 (28-ounce) cans San Marzano tomatoes*, drained, juice reserved
- 2 teaspoons salt
- 2 teaspoons sugar
- 1 teaspoon crushed red pepper flakes
- 8 to 12 ounces spaghetti noodles
  Freshly grated Parmesan cheese, to taste
- 10 fresh whole basil leaves

Make the meatballs: Preheat the oven to 350 degrees.

In a large bowl, mix the eggs and the cream and whisk in the salt and pepper. Add the ground chuck, parsley, shallots, and the bread crumbs and mix well.

Line a sheet pan with parchment paper. Scoop and form about 30 (2-inch) balls. Place on the sheet pan lined with parchment paper and roast in the oven for 25 minutes, turning halfway through to brown more evenly. Remove from the oven and let stand until ready to serve.

Prepare the tomato sauce: In a 3- or 4-quart saucepan heat the olive oil over medium heat and sauté the onion and garlic until soft and golden brown, being careful not to burn the garlic. Add the oregano and carrot and continue to sauté until the carrot is soft. Add the juice from the cans of tomatoes. Crush the tomatoes with your hands and add to the pan. Bring the mixture to a simmer, stirring occasionally.

Add the salt, sugar, and crushed red pepper flakes. Continue to simmer for 30 minutes over low heat.

While the sauce is simmering cook the spaghetti according to the package directions. Serve with freshly grated Parmesan cheese and basil leaves.

Serves 6 to 8. Makes 30 to 36 (2-inch) meatballs and 7 cups tomato sauce.

---

* If you can't find San Marzano tomatoes substitute crushed plum tomatoes, but use San Marzano tomatoes to get the full flavor benefit.

Chicken Marsala

A good and easy meal for family or company!

4	chicken breasts (2 whole)	1	teaspoon oregano
1/2	cup flour	2	cups Marsala wine, divided
4	tablespoons olive oil	1	(10-ounce) jar red currant jelly
1	tablespoon minced garlic	1	(16-ounce) carton sour cream
1/2	teaspoon rosemary		Salt and pepper to taste
1/2	teaspoon basil		

Preheat the oven to 350 degrees.

Wash the chicken and pat dry with paper towels. Dust the chicken with the flour.

Heat a 10-inch skillet over medium-high heat and add the oil and garlic, stirring to keep from burning the garlic. Add the chicken breasts; sprinkle them with the rosemary, basil, and oregano; and brown the breasts.

Pour 1 cup of the wine in the skillet, lower the heat, and simmer for 10 minutes.

Remove the chicken from the heat and place in an uncovered 2-quart casserole dish. Pour the sauce from the pan over the chicken and add the remaining wine. Bake for 45 minutes.

In a saucepan or the microwave, melt the currant jelly and add the sour cream. Remove the chicken from the casserole dish and combine the remaining sauce in the baking dish with the jelly mixture. Pour it over the chicken and serve.

This is great served over pasta too.

Serves 4.

SMOKY CHIPOTLE GRILLED BABY BACK RIBS

Ribs are one of my favorite meals. It doesn't have to be July 4 to enjoy them. I don't like a sauce that takes my breath away, but the chipotle peppers give this a good medium heat without taking your head off. If you like your sauce spicy, add another 1/2 to whole pepper.

The ribs:

- 2 (3 1/2- to 4-pound) slabs baby back ribs
- 1 1/2 cups apple cider
- 1 cup water

The rub:

- 2 tablespoons packed brown sugar
- 2 teaspoons salt
- 2 teaspoons garlic salt
- 1 tablespoon chili powder
- 1 tablespoon paprika
- 2 teaspoons black pepper

The sauce:

- 1 (28-ounce) can crushed tomatoes
- 1/2 cup honey
- 1/2 cup light brown sugar
- 2 chipotle peppers in adobo, minced
- 1/2 sweet onion, chopped
- 1/2 cup apple cider vinegar
- 1/2 cup apple cider
- 3 limes, juiced
- 4 cloves garlic, minced
- 1 1/2 tablespoons dry mustard
- 2 teaspoons salt
- 1 teaspoon black pepper
- 1 teaspoon cumin

Preheat the oven to 325 degrees.

Use a knife to loosen and peel the membrane from the back of the ribs if still attached. Rinse the ribs and pat dry with a paper towel. Place them in a roasting pan. In a small bowl mix the apple cider and water and pour the mixture into the bottom of the pan.

In a small bowl combine the brown sugar, salt, garlic salt, chili powder, paprika, and black pepper. Sprinkle the rub over the ribs, coating them heavily.

Cover the roasting pan with aluminum foil and roast the ribs in the preheated oven for 2 hours.

While the ribs are roasting, put the tomatoes and juice in a heavy medium-size saucepan. Using your hands, crush the tomatoes into smaller pieces. Add the honey, brown sugar, chipotle peppers, onion, apple cider vinegar, apple cider, lime juice, garlic, dry mustard, salt, pepper, and cumin, stirring to blend well, and bring to a boil. Lower the heat and simmer 40 minutes, stirring 2 to 3 times. Sauce should be reduced and thickened.

Preheat a gas or charcoal grill. The heat is correct when you can hold your hand 3 to 4 inches over the grate for no more than 5 seconds. Remove the ribs from the oven and brush both sides of the ribs with the sauce. Grill the ribs, meat side down, for 10 to 15 minutes, basting several times. Brush the top side of the ribs with sauce and turn bone side down. Heavily baste the top (meat) side and close the grill cover. Cook for another 10 minutes, basting often.

Remove the ribs from the grill, cut into serving-size pieces, and serve with the remaining sauce.

Serves 4 to 6.

TIP: The sauce will keep in the refrigerator for 10 to 14 days.

ALTERNATE COOKING METHOD: If you don't want to use a grill, preheat the broiler. Place the ribs on a foil-lined baking sheet. Brush both sides of the ribs with the sauce and cook 4 to 5 minutes, 6 to 8 inches from the heating element, until the sauce caramelizes, being careful not to burn it.

MARINATED PORK TENDERLOIN

Andy and Erika Riddle shared this recipe with me. They love to spend time together in the kitchen cooking for family and friends. This marinade keeps it simple. Pair the pork with an assortment of fresh grilled vegetables. Include some sliced sweet potatoes dusted with brown sugar.

1 cup soy sauce	1 (2-pack) package pork tenderloins
1 cup packed brown sugar	

In a zip-top plastic bag, mix the soy sauce and brown sugar. Zip the bag closed and shake to mix and dissolve the sugar. Put the tenderloins in the bag and let marinate overnight, turning as often as you can.

When ready to cook, remove the tenderloins and discard the marinade.

Preheat a gas or charcoal grill to medium-hot. The heat is correct when you can hold your hand 5 inches above the grate for no more than 3 or 4 seconds. Oil the grates. Place the tenderloins on the grill and cook, turning frequently, until an instant-read thermometer inserted diagonally 2 inches into the meat registers 150 degrees, about 20 minutes.

Transfer to a cutting board and tent loosely with foil. Let stand 5 to 10 minutes before slicing. Cooking to this temperature and tenting the pork to further cook should ensure that the pork is moist and delicious.

Serves 8.

CHICKEN NIKO

A delicious recipe from Mary Miltiades of Magnolia Moments Catering.

6	boneless chicken breast halves	6	slices deli ham, cut into bite-size pieces
1	cup flour		
2	tablespoons Parmesan cheese	2	zucchini, sliced
1/2	teaspoon salt	8	mushrooms, sliced
1/2	teaspoon pepper	1	onion, chopped
1	teaspoon parsley	1	teaspoon basil
1/2	teaspoon garlic powder	2	cloves fresh garlic, chopped
2	teaspoons dried oregano, divided	3/4	cup sun-dried tomatoes
1/2	cup milk	1/2	cup butter
2	tablespoons olive oil	8	ounces mozzarella cheese, shredded
	Nonstick cooking spray		

Place the chicken breasts between plastic wrap and pound slightly with a meat tenderizer. On a plate, mix the flour, Parmesan cheese, salt, pepper, parsley, garlic powder, and 1 teaspoon of the oregano.

Pour the milk into a small bowl and dip the breasts first in the milk and then in the flour. Set aside.

Heat a large sauté pan on medium-high heat and add the olive oil. Sauté each breast until a nice golden brown color. Place in a 13 x 9-inch baking dish that has been sprayed with a nonstick spray. Top with the ham.

Sauté the zucchini, mushrooms, and onions in the pan drippings. Add the basil, garlic, the remaining oregano, sun-dried tomatoes, and butter. Heat and pour over the chicken.

Top with the mozzarella cheese. Bake for 20 to 30 minutes until the cheese is melted.

Serves 6.

LIVE TO EAT, EAT TO LIVE, LIVE TO COOK

Our Creator designed us with a need for physical food to sustain our bodies. I believe that finding pleasure and comfort in eating good food is a God-ordained gift. Some of us complicate the issue by the extent to which we take it. I am a person who can obsess at times over what my next meal is going to consist of or what I will next use for comfort food. In the past I suffered from the delusion that there are only two kinds of people in this world in reference to our relationship with food: *people who eat to live* and *people who live to eat*.

I have often been envious of people who operate in the "eat to live" category, but I have expanded my observations and now realize there is another group: *people who live to cook*. Some contributors to this book operate in that "live to cook" mode the majority of the time. They have been generous in sharing the fruits of their labor with me, and I, in turn, share these gems with you.

On special family occasions, when I entertain, and on the few rare occasions that I now get to cook at the store, I find myself in the "live

Debbie Willyard, good friend and chef for the photo shoot.

to cook" mode. Made in the image of our Creator, we desire to nourish and comfort those we love and care about. Preparing food is one way we can give to and comfort others—it is a form of art and creativity for many of us. The recent popularity of the science and art of cooking, evidenced by the many television channels and programs devoted totally to food, tells me that while all of us can't be painters, sculptors, or potters, we *can* all learn to cook. We imitate and reflect our Creator in that we nourish and comfort and create as He does—we just do it with food!

Autumn Root Vegetable Gratin (page 122)

SIDES

COUSCOUS
WITH GRILLED VEGETABLES

Alexis and Greg Amaden are two talented and hospitable Marietta hosts. As the Innkeeper of the Whitlock Inn, Lexie (as she is called by friends), gets plenty of practice. She created this dish using leftovers from wedding receptions. Serve it hot or cold as a vegetarian picnic entrée or add grilled chicken.* Add other vegetables such as red or green peppers for a very colorful mix.

1/4	cup chopped fresh oregano	1	red onion
1/4	cup chopped fresh parsley	2	zucchini
	Juice of 2 lemons	2	yellow squash
3	tablespoons olive oil	1	(10-ounce) package couscous
1	tablespoon water	1/2	cup pistachios
2 to 3	cloves garlic, minced	3	Roma tomatoes, chopped

In a small bowl add the oregano, parsley, lemon juice, olive oil, water, and garlic. Stir to combine.

Preheat a gas or stovetop grill to medium high. Cut the onion, zucchini, and squash into fairly large pieces and brush with the prepared vinaigrette mixture.* Place the vegetables on the grill, flesh side down, and grill for 10 minutes, turning as necessary to prevent burning. Allow the vegetables to cool until they're comfortable to handle.

While the vegetables are cooling prepare the couscous according to package directions.**

Cut the cooled vegetables into coin-size pieces and add them to a large bowl. Add the couscous, pistachios, tomatoes, and remaining vinaigrette, and stir to combine.

Serves 6 to 8.

* Make a separate container of the vinaigrette to brush on the chicken. Discard leftover vinaigrette that comes into contact with raw chicken.

** Do not use the spice mix that might be included in the packaged couscous.

AUTUMN ROOT VEGETABLE GRATIN

This is another great recipe from Tom McEachern, the executive chef at Ray's on the River in Atlanta. Having dinner at Tom's house or at Ray's is a dining phenomenon. The true goodness and flavors of the food he prepares are not changed by his preparation, just enhanced!

1	tablespoon unsalted butter	2	medium gold beets, peeled and cut into 1/4-inch slices
2	cups heavy cream		
1	head garlic, cut in half	3	medium turnips, peeled and cut into 1/4-inch slices
2	sprigs fresh rosemary		
	Salt and pepper to taste	1	medium butternut squash, peeled, seeded, and cut into 1/4-inch slices
1	medium red beet, peeled and cut into 1/4-inch slices		
2	large sweet potatoes, peeled and cut into 1/4-inch slices	1 1/2	cups grated Parmesan cheese

Preheat the oven to 375 degrees. Grease a porcelain 13 x 9-inch dish or a large porcelain soufflé dish with butter and set aside.

In a medium saucepan bring the cream, garlic, and rosemary to a simmer. Add salt and pepper to taste. Simmer for 10 minutes, or until the mixture is slightly thickened. Strain and reserve the cream.

Layer the vegetables in the greased dish, starting with the red beet and ending with the butternut squash. Continue layering each vegetable as desired, adding a little salt and pepper to each layer. (You may not be able to use all of the slices depending on the size of your dish.) Be sure to leave at least 2 inches of space at the top of the dish so that it doesn't spill over in the oven.

Pour the garlic-rosemary cream over the layers, filling the dish just 1/3 of the way. (You may not be able to use all of the cream.) Cover tightly with aluminum foil and place on a heavy sheet pan to protect the oven from any spillover.

Bake in the oven for 30 to 45 minutes, or until each layer is easily pierced with a knife.

Remove the aluminum foil, sprinkle with Parmesan cheese, and return to the oven for 10 to 15 minutes, or until golden brown.

Serves 10 to 12.

TIP: The red beet will give this dish a lot of color, but placing it on the bottom will prevent the dish from having too much of that color.

TIP: Substitute other seasonal root vegetables, if you desire.

CAULIFLOWER AU GRATIN

I don't know about you, but I have a hard time finding recipes with cauliflower that I love. But this one, from Chef Tom McEachern, is a good one.

1 pound cauliflower	1 1/3 cups Béchamel sauce (page 234)
4 ounces cheddar cheese, medium dice	Salt and pepper to taste
	1 teaspoon butter

Preheat the oven to 350 degrees and place a large pot of water on the stove and bring to a boil.

Break off the green exterior leaves of the cauliflower, and discard. Wash the cauliflower and break it into individual florets. Add the florets to the boiling water and blanch* for 10 minutes, or until they begin to soften. Remove the florets with a strainer and place them in a 13 x 9-inch pan.

In a medium bowl add the cheddar cheese, Béchamel sauce, salt, pepper, and butter. Mix well and pour over the cauliflower. Cover with aluminum foil and bake for 15 minutes.

Serves 8.

* See the glossary on page 267 for blanching tips.

SOUTHERN GRITS
WITH ARTICHOKE CHEESE SAUCE

Mary Miltiades, the owner of Magnolia Moments catering, gave me this recipe. I had it one evening at a party her company catered. I think this is possibly one of the best grits dishes I have ever tasted.

Grits:

3	cups water
1	tablespoon chicken granules
1	teaspoon salt
1/2	teaspoon Tabasco sauce
1	cup Aunt Jemima Quick Grits (red package)
1	cup heavy whipping cream
1	cup shredded Mexican cheese blend

Topping:

2	ounces melted butter
1	(6-ounce) jar sliced mushrooms, drained
1	(14-ounce) can artichoke hearts, quartered and drained
1	(2-ounce) jar pimientos, drained
2	tablespoons dried minced onions
1	tablespoon lemon pepper
1	teaspoon dry mustard
1	teaspoon garlic powder
1	(15-ounce) jar salsa con queso cheese sauce
1	cup shredded Mexican cheese blend
1/2 to 3/4 cup grated Parmesan cheese	

Make the grits: In a medium saucepan bring the water to a boil. Add the chicken granules, salt, Tabasco, and grits. Cook for 3 minutes and remove from the heat. Cover and let sit for 15 minutes.

Preheat the oven to 350 degrees.

Add the cream and the cheese to the grits. Pour into a greased 13 x 9-inch baking dish. Set aside while you prepare the topping.

Prepare the topping: In a medium bowl combine the butter, mushrooms, artichoke hearts, pimientos, onions, lemon pepper, dry mustard, garlic powder, salsa con queso sauce, and Mexican cheese. Pour the topping over the grits. Sprinkle with the Parmesan cheese and bake for 35 to 40 minutes.

Serves 12 to 14.

* Substitute 3 cups of chicken stock for the water and granules if you don't have the granules. Substituting chicken stock or cream when cooking grits only enhances the flavor.

COLESLAW THE EASY WAY

Even if you eat out 14 days in a row and have coleslaw each time, the only thing each one might have in common is the cabbage. I never thought of cabbage as a versatile food, but the more places I have coleslaw, the more possibilities I see. My Bible study friend Gail Schwartz brought this delicious coleslaw to our Christmas dinner. We practically licked the bowl!

1	package angel hair coleslaw mix*	Garlic salt with parsley to taste
1	carton cherry tomatoes, halved	Capers to taste
4	tablespoon dried chives	Hellman's mayonnaise to taste

In a large bowl add the coleslaw mix, halved tomatoes, chives, garlic salt, capers, and mayonnaise and mix well. Chill for 15 to 20 minutes.

Serves 4 to 6.

SERVING TIP: We all know that coleslaw is good on a hot dog, but it's good on a sandwich as well. I love it on a crab cake or turkey sandwich. Of course, serving it with pinto beans or a fresh vegetable plate is a classic that Southerners love.

---

* You can substitute 1/2 head of finely shredded cabbage that has been rinsed and drained for the angel hair coleslaw mix.

Southern Vegetable Pie

This beautiful dish combines two of my favorites: vegetables and cream cheese.

3	tablespoons extra-virgin oil		Heavy duty aluminum foil
1½	cups sliced leeks		Nonstick cooking spray
3	cloves garlic, minced	6	large eggs
3	medium yellow squash, sliced ¼-inch thick	¼	cup heavy cream
		2	teaspoons salt
3	medium zucchini, sliced ¼-inch thick	1	tablespoon chopped basil
1	each red, yellow, and green bell pepper, seeded and sliced into ¼-inch-wide strips	2	teaspoons freshly ground pepper
		2	cups ½-inch cubes stale French bread
8	ounces baby bella mushrooms	8	ounces cream cheese, diced
3	cups baby spinach	10	ounces Manchego, Swiss, or Gouda cheese, shredded (2 cups)

Preheat the oven to 350 degrees. In a large skillet add the olive oil and sauté the leeks and garlic over medium heat, until the leeks are soft. Add yellow squash, zucchini, bell peppers, and mushrooms and sauté until crisp-tender, 15 to 20 minutes. Remove from the heat and fold in the baby spinach. The spinach will wilt with residual heat. Set aside to cool to room temperature.

Line a 10-inch springform pan with foil and spray with nonstick spray. Press the foil flat and smooth against the sides of the pan.

In a large bowl whisk the eggs and cream together and season with salt, pepper, and basil. Stir in the bread cubes and cheeses. Combine the egg mixture with the sautéed vegetables and stir until well combined. Pour into the greased 10-inch springform pan and pack the mixture tightly.

Place the springform pan on a baking sheet. Bake the pie for 1 hour, until it becomes puffed and golden brown and is firm to the touch. If the top browns too quickly, cover with aluminum foil. Serve hot, cold, or at room temperature.

Serves 8 to 10.

NOTE: If you don't have a springform pan you can use a 4-inch-high x 10-inch-wide cake pan, sprayed with nonstick spray.

GRATIN DAUPHINOIS
(POTATOES, MUSHROOMS, AND CHEESE)

Mary Gillis is one of those natural cooks. She can take two or three recipes, put them all together, and come up with something delicious. I envy that. Try these. They are delicious!

8	cups thinly sliced potatoes	1/4	cup melted butter, divided
1	teaspoon salt	1 to 1 1/2	pounds sliced mushrooms
1/4	teaspoon pepper	8	ounces Jarlsberg cheese, grated
1	clove garlic, freshly minced	2	eggs, beaten
1/8	teaspoon nutmeg	2	cups whipping cream
		2	tablespoons fresh Parmesan

Preheat the oven to 350 degrees.

In a large bowl toss the potatoes, salt, pepper, garlic, nutmeg, and 1/4 cup of the butter. Set aside.

In a shallow greased gratin pan or 13 x 9-inch baking dish, layer half of the potato slices. Top with half of the mushroom. Sprinkle with half of the Jarlsberg cheese. Repeat the layers. In a medium bowl mix the eggs and cream. Pour over the layers. Top with Parmesan cheese. Cover with aluminum foil and bake for 50 to 60 minutes. Remove cover and bake until lightly browned. Insert a fork into the potatoes to make sure they are cooked through.

Serves 10 to 12.

---

* Mushrooms release their juices when they are cooked, so start with just 1 tablespoon butter. Add the other tablespoon if necessary.

GREEN BEANS WITH CRISPY BACON, MUSHROOMS, AND SHALLOTS

Another good addition to a meal by Mary Gillis.

Ice cubes	2 medium-large shallots, halved lengthwise and very thinly sliced
1 to 2 teaspoons plus 1/4 teaspoon salt, divided	1/4 cup very thinly sliced sage leaves
2 pounds green beans, trimmed	2 tablespoons white balsamic vinegar
Paper towels	1 teaspoon cream sherry
8 ounces sliced bacon	1 teaspoon Dijon mustard
3 tablespoons olive oil, divided	
1 (6-ounce) package baby bellas, cut in half and thinly sliced	

Fill a large mixing bowl with ice cubes and water. Set aside.

Fill a 7-quart stockpot two-thirds full of water. Bring the water to a boil and add 1 to 2 teaspoons of the salt. Add the beans and boil uncovered until tender to the bite, 4 to 6 minutes. Drain, transfer to the bowl of ice water, and let sit until cooled, about 2 minutes. Drain in a colander and pat dry with paper towels.

In a large skillet cook the bacon over medium heat until crisp and browned. Remove from the pan and allow to drain on a paper towel–lined plate. When cool, crumble and set aside. Remove the pan from the heat and let it cool down.

Add 2 tablespoons of the olive oil to the pan and return to the stove over medium-high heat. Add the mushrooms, shallots, and 1/4 teaspoon salt and cook, stirring, unto browned, about 5 minutes. Add the sage and stir for an additional 30 seconds. Remove the pan from the heat and add the vinegar, cream sherry, mustard, and the remaining tablespoon of oil. Whisk to blend well.

Return the pan to medium heat, add the green beans and stir to coat with the warm dressing. Season with salt and pepper. Heat for 2 to 3 minutes, until beans are hot. Transfer to a warmed serving dish and garnish with bacon.

Serves 8 to 10.

TIP: Prepare the green beans ahead and store in the refrigerator. Allow the beans to come to room temperature an hour before you're ready to finish the dish.

MAPLE GARLIC–GLAZED GREEN BEANS

Debbie Willyard, my chef friend, says that this recipe will make you want to never eat green beans without maple syrup again. I can't think of anything that wouldn't be good with butter and syrup . . . Try them and let me know what you think.

4 to 5 cups water
1   pound fresh green beans*
2   tablespoons salt
1/4 cup butter

1   clove garlic, minced
    Salt and pepper to taste
3   tablespoons pure maple syrup

In a large saucepan bring the water to a boil.

Wash the beans and snap off the stems.

When the water begins to boil, add the salt and stir. Add the beans to the salted water and boil them until they begin to soften.** Strain the beans and rinse them in cold water. Set aside.

In a medium sauté pan melt the butter over medium heat. Add the garlic and the strained beans to the pan. Add salt and black pepper to taste. Add the maple syrup and stir to coat the beans. Serve immediately.

Serves 4.

* Don't use pole beans for this recipe. They are too tough.

** Do not allow the beans to get mushy.

HERBED TOMATO BREAD PUDDING

One of our chefs, Jessica Jacobs, is just a whiz at putting together sweet and savory bread puddings. She also has a sweet potato bread pudding on page 212. This is one of my favorite savory dishes.

2	tablespoons blended olive oil or extra-virgin olive oil	8	eggs
3	cups medium diced* yellow onion	16	ounces heavy whipping cream
2/3	cup celery	4	ounces mozzarella, shredded
3	tablespoons garlic	8	ounces chicken stock
1/2	cup roasted red peppers, chopped	6	ounces milk
1	tablespoon dried rosemary	1	(16-ounce) can stewed tomatoes
2	ounces chicken sausage	1	pound old bread
3	tablespoons dried basil		Nonstick cooking spray

Preheat the oven to 350 degrees.

Preheat a medium sauté pan over medium-high heat. When the pan gets hot add the olive oil, onion, and celery. Sauté until the onions are translucent. Add the garlic, roasted red peppers, rosemary, chicken sausage, and basil. Sauté about 5 minutes. Remove from the heat and cool.

In a large bowl whisk together the eggs and heavy cream. Add the cheese, chicken stock, and milk.

Combine the cooked mixture with the stewed tomatoes. Add to the egg mixture. Add the bread and combine well.

Spray a 9 x 13-inch pan and add the mixture to the pan.

Bake uncovered for about 30 minutes.

Serves 14 to 18.

NOTE: The bread pudding mixture may be frozen and baked at a later time.

* See the glossary for tips on getting the perfect dice on your vegetables every time.

DANISH RED CABBAGE

This recipe was shared by Sandra Pontius, a really good Marietta cook. She and her sister, Kitty O'Keefe in Minneapolis, Minnesota, make this dish at Easter to serve with ham. She suggests cooking the cabbage the day before to keep your house from smelling like cabbage on the day you serve it.

1	head red cabbage	1/3	cup white vinegar
4	tablespoons butter	1/4	cup red currant jelly
1	tablespoon sugar	2	tablespoons grated apple
1/2	teaspoon salt	1	(10.5-ounce) package goat cheese, crumbled
1/3	cup water		

Preheat the oven to 325 degrees.

Remove the outer layers and the core of the cabbage. Cut in half from top to bottom. Cut each half into thin slices.

In a large pot bring the butter, sugar, salt, water, and vinegar to a boil. Add the cabbage, and toss it to thoroughly coat with the liquid. Bring to a boil again. Transfer to a greased 13 x 9-inch pan and cover tightly. Bake for 2 hours at 325 degrees.

Stir in the jelly and apple. Bake 10 more minutes. Add more jelly if you prefer cabbage a little sweeter. Remove from the oven and serve immediately or place in a tightly sealed container and refrigerate.

Reheat in the oven when ready to serve, 15 to 20 minutes until hot. Add the goat cheese during the last 5 minutes of cooking.

Serves 6 to 8.

MOCK SPINACH SOUFFLE
OR BAKED CREAMED SPINACH

Debbie Willyard is a wife, mother, grandmother, and a trained chef. After twenty years as a paralegal, Debbie decided to go to culinary school. I am sure glad she did. Debbie worked as the chef on the photo shoot for Second Helpings, *and we have done a couple of other events together. This lady knows what she's doing when she gets in the kitchen! This mock spinach soufflé is one of her mom's recipes. When Debbie was growing up, her mom doctored up the vegetables to get Debbie to eat them. This recipe is super-easy to put together and goes great with sautéed fish or chicken.*

2	(10-ounce) packages frozen chopped spinach, thawed	2	green onions, chopped white and green parts
2	tablespoons butter	1/4	teaspoon kosher salt
1	clove garlic, minced	1/2	teaspoon pepper
1/2	cup heavy whipping cream	1/2	cup grated Parmesan cheese
1	egg		Nonstick cooking spray
1/2	teaspoon nutmeg		

Preheat the oven to 350 degrees.

Squeeze all the water out of the thawed spinach and set aside.

In a small microwave-safe bowl, melt the butter with the minced garlic for about 30 seconds, or until the butter is bubbly. Set aside.

In a large mixing bowl, whisk the heavy whipping cream, egg, butter mixture, nutmeg, chopped green onions, salt, and pepper. Stir in the spinach and combine. Stir in the Parmesan cheese.*

Bake in a sprayed 8 x 8-inch baking dish for 20 minutes.

Serves 6 to 8.

* Parmesan cheese has a lot of salt in it, so you can use less salt and still be flavorful.

POTATOES AND BEER

Liz Cole is such a great cook! I don't think you can have too many potato recipes.

6	medium potatoes, unpeeled	5	tablespoons butter
1	large sweet onion, thinly sliced	2	cups beer
8	slices bacon, cooked and crumbled, divided	1	cup heavy whipping cream
	Salt and pepper to taste	3	tablespoons chopped fresh chives
			Paprika

Preheat the oven to 350 degrees. Butter a 13 x 9-inch baking dish.

Wash the potatoes but don't peel them. Thinly slice the potatoes and layer them with the onion slices and half of the bacon in the casserole dish. Add salt and pepper to each layer and dot with butter. Pour the beer over the potatoes. Cover the dish with foil and bake for 30 minutes.

Remove the dish from the oven. Uncover and pour the heavy whipping cream over the potatoes and bake uncovered for 30 more minutes.

Drop chopped chives and the remaining bacon on top and sprinkle with paprika for color. Serve hot.

Serves 8.

RED POTATO AND VEGETABLE HASH

You know it's a winner if Tom McEachern serves it at Ray's on the River in Atlanta. Ed and I thought this dish was so tasty we didn't want any to go to waste. We decided to make a Red Potato Vegetable Frittata with the leftovers. Check it out on page 147.

1	(2-pound) bag red potatoes	1/2	cup small-diced red pepper
1	bunch asparagus	1/2	cup small-diced yellow pepper
2	tablespoons olive oil	1/2	cup small-diced green pepper
	Salt and pepper to taste	1	cup yellow corn kernels
1/2	cup small-diced* yellow onion		

Place whole, unpeeled potatoes in a medium saucepan and cover with water. Bring to a boil and boil for 5 minutes, cooking until al dente.** Drain potatoes in a colander and set aside to cool.

Bring a medium saucepan filled about three-fourths full of water to a rolling boil. Drop the asparagus in and lightly blanch for about 1 minute. Rinse in cold water, drain, and set aside.

Cut the potatoes into a 1/4-inch dice. Heat a large skillet on high until hot and add the olive oil. Add the potatoes and sauté until they have a nice brown color. Don't stir too much or they will get mushy instead of browning. Add salt and pepper to taste. When the potatoes are browned, turn the heat down to medium and add the diced onion to the pan. Sauté the onions and potatoes until the onions are translucent, about 5 minutes. While the potatoes and onions are cooking, cut the cooled asparagus spears on the diagonal into 1 1/2-inch pieces.

When the potato and onion mixture is ready, add the peppers, asparagus, and corn. Sauté and stir just enough to slightly cook the added vegetables and heat them through (peppers cook really fast). Taste and add more salt and pepper, if needed. Serve immediately.

Serves 6.

* Cubed into 1/4-inch pieces.

** See glossary on page 267 for tips to preparing foods al dente.

SCALLOPED PINEAPPLE

Estelle Bogle, a great Marietta cook, remembers getting this recipe from another fun-loving Marietta hostess, the late Betsy Lee Holladay. It's in Estelle's collection of favorites.

1	cup butter	2	(20-ounce) cans pineapple chunks, save the juice from 1½ cans
1½	cups sugar	½	cup cream
2	eggs	1	quart packed bread cubes*

Preheat the oven to 350 degrees.

In a mixing bowl cream the butter and sugar. Add the eggs and beat well. Add the pineapple chunks, juice, cream, and bread cubes. Pour the mixture into a 2-quart casserole dish and bake for 1 hour.

Serves 8 to 10.

* Estelle uses 8 to 10 slices of Pepperidge Farm Toasting Bread with crusts removed.

SQUASH CASSEROLE

This is just one of the squash dishes that Evelyn Elliott has in her arsenal to keep her family well fed. Enjoy!

2	pounds squash, cooked in water, drained and mashed up	1	(10.75-ounce) can cream of chicken soup*
2	carrots, finely grated	1	cup sour cream
1	onion, diced	1	stick margarine
1	small jar pimientos, drained	1	package stuffing mix
			Nonstick cooking spray

Preheat the oven to 350 degrees.

In a boiler, cover the squash, carrots, and onions with water and cook until tender, about 10 to 15 minutes. Drain the vegetables in a colander.

In a large bowl add the vegetables, pimientos, soup, and sour cream and combine well.

In a medium microwave-proof bowl, melt the margarine. Add the stuffing mix to the melted margarine.

Spray a 13 x 9-inch baking dish with nonstick cooking spray. Spread half of the stuffing mix over the bottom of the baking dish in an even layer. Spread the squash over the stuffing mix and cover the squash with the remaining stuffing. Bake for 30 minutes.

Serves 12.

* Evelyn rinses out the can with a little water and adds it to the soup.

Sweet Potato Fries

This recipe is just delicious. Andrew Smith worked at Gabriel's for a while and made these for us one afternoon. We all went crazy over them. They're the best!

4	sweet potatoes, peeled and cut (French fry cut)	3	cups vegetable oil
	Salt and pepper to taste	1/4	cup brown sugar
1	cup all-purpose flour	3 to 4	ounces butter, room temperature

Put the cut potatoes in a large bowl and sprinkle with salt and pepper to taste. Sift the flour over the fries and add water to the mixture until a paste forms. The batter should stick to the fries but not be runny.

Preheat a deep fat fryer half full of vegetable oil to 375 degrees. Carefully place the potatoes in the hot oil and cook until lightly browned.

Remove from the oil and toss in a bowl with the brown sugar and butter, coating evenly. Serve immediately.

Serves 6 to 8.

ALTERNATE COOKING METHOD: Add 3 inches of vegetable oil to a large skillet and preheat to 375 degrees over medium-high heat.

John Elliott's Soon-to-Be-World-Famous Tomato Pie

John Elliott has two recipes in his repertoire. This is one of them. He can hardly wait for fresh tomatoes to come into season every year so he can make this delicious, low-fat dish.

2	cups mozzarella cheese, shredded and divided		Salt and pepper to taste
1	(9-inch) deep dish pie shell		Oregano or Italian seasoning to taste
1	large sweet onion, thinly sliced and halved	2	large or 3 medium tomatoes, sliced
		6 to 8	fresh basil leaves, julienned

Preheat the oven to 375 degrees.

Sprinkle 1/4 cup of the mozzarella cheese in the bottom of the uncooked pie shell. Layer half of the ingredients in the following order: onions, salt and pepper, oregano, 1/2 cup mozzarella cheese, tomato slices, and fresh basil.

Create another layer in the same order. Sprinkle the remaining 3/4 cup mozzarella cheese on top and bake for 1 hour.

Cover loosely with aluminum foil if pie crust edges and cheese begin to brown too much.

Serves 6 to 8.

NOTE: While fresh tomatoes will give this dish the best flavor, you can make this pie year-round with store-bought tomatoes.

WILD RICE AND CORN SALAD

Estelle Bogle is a great hostess. She exudes energy and life, and her parties show it. Estelle suggests pork tenderloin or fish with this salad.

1	cup cooked wild rice (not a wild rice mix)	3	green onions, thinly sliced
2	(11-ounce) cans white shoepeg corn, rinsed and drained	1	(8-ounce) can water chestnuts, drained and chopped
1/2	cup mayonnaise	1/4	teaspoon salt
		1/8	teaspoon pepper

In a medium bowl mix the wild rice, corn, mayonnaise, green onions, water chestnuts, salt, and pepper.

Cover and chill for at least 2 hours. Keeps well in the refrigerator 2 to 3 days.

Serves 8 to 10.

Evelyn Elliott, the matriarch of Southern cooks, prepares her squash this way. I was fortunate enough to sit at her table when she served her family this dish, along with her fried chicken, macaroni and cheese, and homemade biscuits, just to name a few. It reminds me of the squash I ate at my grandmother's table. Evelyn's squash casserole is on page 141 but this is for the squash purist.

6	slices bacon	1	large onion, diced
2	pounds yellow squash, washed and cut into pieces		Salt and pepper to taste
			Nonstick cooking spray

Preheat the oven to 350 degrees.

In a medium skillet cook the bacon until crisp. Remove the bacon from the pan and drain on paper towels. Do not discard the bacon grease in the pan. Place the squash and onions in a boiler with salt and pepper to taste, adding enough water to almost cover. Bring to a boil and lower the heat. Simmer uncovered until tender. There should still be some water remaining.

Stir in some of the bacon grease to taste, and cook on low heat until most of the water is gone. The squash shouldn't be greasy from the bacon drippings.

Spray a 13 x 9-inch casserole dish with nonstick spray and pour the squash mixture into the dish. Sprinkle the chopped bacon on top and cook in the oven for 20 minutes.*

Serves 8.

* The squash should still be moist. Do not allow it to get dried out.

RED POTATO
VEGETABLE HASH FRITTATA

The vegetable hash on page 139 was so tasty I thought it would be a shame for any to be wasted. I turned the leftovers into this frittata. Try it and see what you think.

1½ teaspoons olive oil
1½ to 2 cups leftover red potato vegetable hash (page 139)
3 large eggs
6 large egg whites*
½ teaspoon salt

¼ teaspoon ground black pepper
1 ounce Asiago, Parmesan, or Reggiano cheese, grated
1 cup chopped tomatoes
1 tablespoon chopped fresh basil or 1½ teaspoons dried basil

Preheat the broiler. In a 10-inch ovenproof nonstick skillet heat the olive oil. Add the vegetable hash and heat through to warm.

In a medium bowl whisk the eggs, whites, salt, and pepper until well blended. Pour the egg mixture over the hash in the skillet and stir gently. Reduce heat to medium-low. Cook without stirring until the eggs are set, about 5 minutes.

Sprinkle the cheese over the frittata and place in the oven to melt the cheese. Sprinkle with tomatoes and basil.

Serves 4.

NOTE: Serve this frittata with a fruit salad for a great brunch.

* I used the pasteurized whites in the carton.

MEN AND WHOOPIE PIES

When did you first hear of whoopie pies? Did you eat them as a child growing up? Did your mother or grandmother make them for you? Why do we always ask if it was your mother or your grandmother? In my young days my dad or grandfather didn't cook anything but eggs and bacon and in later years cooked on a charcoal grill—but only the meat on a grill, certainly not vegetables! The next generation will be asking, "Did your mom or dad . . ." or in a couple of generations "Did your granddad or grandmother cook you so and so?" I think it is great that dads are spending time in the kitchen—and loving it. It's a new area for family togetherness.

Nevertheless, I'm curious as to whether everyone except me grew up eating whoopie pies. The closest thing to a whoopie pie in my household was a Moon Pie—and those were rare because Mom didn't buy many desserts. She would pick up a bag of Oreos for Dad just in case we ran out of Big Mama's pound cake.

Daddy always had to have dessert after his supper of a meat, two vegetables, and biscuits. I can't even imagine Dad's reaction if Mom had offered him a Moon Pie for

dessert. It was pretty amazing that he learned to eat a canned biscuit. He was a kind and gentle man, who knew Mom worked hard outside the home, so eating a canned biscuit was one thing he would concede to because he certainly wasn't going to learn to cook! Daddy did lots of work in the yard; he wasn't lazy. Those were the days in Macon when men often watered the grass by hand with a water hose. Standing outside watering the grass—a lawn that he had hand sprigged—kept him out of a house of all women.

Now that I have been exposed to homemade whoopie pies, I believe Daddy would have been happy to eat one for dessert with his sweet ice tea (he never gained a pound). Mo Bednarowski, our catering manager, introduced me to whoopie pies—chocolate and pumpkin flavors. Both of the recipes are in this cookbook. When I eat the chocolate, they're my favorite, and when Mo makes the pumpkin ones, they're my favorite.

Then there are the red velvet whoopee pies! *You-know-who* has made that one famous. When Paula asked me to contribute recipes for her family cookbook, knowing that Paula and especially Michael love the red velvet cupcake, which is already in *Cooking in the South*, we came up with a recipe for the whoopie pie in red velvet (see *The Deen Family Cookbook*). We submitted the recipe to her, along with several others. She used them all, I think, but she rarely fails to mention the red velvet cupcake or the whoopie pie, and usually both, if she's anywhere near Atlanta, Marietta, the state of Georgia, or anytime the two of us are together. I learned to never show up without them on a visit to see Paula.

I had always heard of the wonders of an RC cola and a Moon Pie. I am thinking a three-vegetable plate of fried okra, creamed corn, and turnip greens topped off with a whoopie pie just might become a new Southern legend.

Caramel Pecan Apple Pie (page 194)

DESSERTS

APPLE PECAN
AND CARAMEL CHEESECAKE

This cheesecake is delicious and worth the extra steps.

Crust:

3 cups graham cracker crumbs (22 whole crackers)

1/4 cup sugar

9 tablespoons butter, melted

Filling:

2 pounds cream cheese, room temperature

1 1/2 cups sugar

2 tablespoons cornstarch

16 ounces sour cream

1/2 cup orange juice

1/2 teaspoon vanilla extract

4 jumbo eggs

Topping:

1/2 cup plus 1 tablespoon butter, divided

1 1/2 pounds golden delicious apples, peeled and cut into 1/2-inch cubes

1/2 cup chopped pecans

1 cup sugar

1/2 cup whipping cream

Make the crust: Preheat the oven to 350 degrees. In a food processor mix the graham cracker crumbs, sugar, and butter until a coarse mixture forms.

Press the mixture onto the bottom and up the sides of a 10-inch springform pan. Bake for 10 minutes. Remove from the oven and cool completely.

Make the filling: In a food processor or upright mixer, mix the cream cheese, sugar, and cornstarch until smooth. Add the sour cream, orange juice, and vanilla and blend until smooth. Add the eggs one at a time, blending well but not overmixing.

Pour the filling into the cooled crust. Bake until the center moves only slightly when the pan is shaken, about 1 hour and 30 minutes.*

Remove from the oven and cool. Refrigerate overnight.

Cut into serving pieces but don't separate the pieces, leaving the cheesecake in original shape but divided into pieces.

Make the topping: Melt 1/2 cup of the butter in a large skillet over high heat. Add the apples and pecans, stirring until they are coated with butter, about 2 minutes.

Add the sugar, stirring until the sugar dissolves and the liquid comes to a boil, about 3 minutes.

Strain the apples and pecans, reserving the liquid. Return the liquid to the skillet and boil until the liquid turns a medium amber color, stirring often. Remove the skillet from the heat to stop the cooking.

Add the cream and return to the heat, bringing to a boil, whisking constantly. Add the remaining 1 tablespoon butter. Remove from the heat. Add the apples and pecans. Cool until lukewarm.

Spread the apple/caramel mixture evenly over the top of the cheesecake. Refrigerate until ready to serve.

Serves 16.

TIP: Using a knife dipped in hot water before making the slice and then wiping off after each cut will give you a neat, easily sliced cheesecake.

---

* I always bake my cheesecakes in a water bath, which adds 15 to 20 minutes to the baking time. Wrap the bottom of the pan with several layers of aluminum foil to prevent water seeping into the cheesecake. The water should cover the bottom half of the cheesecake pan. Be sure to add the water to the pan after placing the water pan in the oven. Check the water level about an hour into baking, adding water if needed. Be very careful removing the pan from the oven when done.

TRIPLE CHOCOLATE CHEESECAKE

This is the chocolate cheesecake we bake at Gabriel's Desserts. Chocolate of any kind doesn't stay in the display case long, especially chocolate cheesecake!

Chocolate cookie crust:
- 1 1/2 cups chocolate cookie crumbs
- 1/3 cup butter or margarine, melted

Cheesecake:
- 6 ounces semisweet chocolate chips
- 6 ounces milk chocolate chips
- 3 (8-ounce) packages cream cheese, softened
- 1 cup sugar
- 4 eggs
- 1 tablespoon cocoa powder
- 1 tablespoon vanilla extract
- 1 (16-ounce) container of sour cream
- 1 1/2 cups heavy cream, whipped white and or dark chocolate curls if available, for garnish

Preheat the oven to 350 degrees.

Make the chocolate cookie crust: In a medium bowl, combine the cookie crumbs and butter and firmly press the mixture into the bottom of a 10-inch springform pan. Bake 5 to 6 minutes and set aside to cool.

Preheat the oven to 300 degrees.

Make the cheesecake: In the top of a double boiler over low heat, place the semisweet and the milk chocolate chips and heat until chocolate melts.

In a large bowl beat the cream cheese at high speed until light and fluffy. Add the sugar gradually, mixing well. Add the eggs one at a time, mixing after each. Stir in the melted chocolate, cocoa, and vanilla, mixing until well blended. Stir in the sour cream, mixing well but not beating. Pour into the prepared springform pan. Bake for 1 hour and 40 minutes.

The center may still be soft, but the chocolate will firm up when cooled and refrigerated. Cool to room temperature and chill 8 hours or overnight.

When ready to serve, garnish with the whipped cream and chocolate curls.

Serves 12 to 16.

Vanilla Buttercream Frosting

We use this wonderful frosting at Gabriel's for our special-occasion cakes, including wedding cakes.

1	pound plus 1 stick butter (5 sticks total)	1¹/2	(1-pound) boxes confectioners' sugar, sifted (24 ounces)
1¹/4	cups vegetable shortening	1	tablespoon vanilla extract

In a large bowl, with the paddle attachment, beat the butter and shortening until soft. Scrape down the sides and bottom of the bowl. Add the confectioners' sugar in 2 to 3 increments. Scrape down the bowl again, add the vanilla, and whip for about 5 minutes.

When ready to frost a cake: Place one layer, flat side up on a cake plate and with an offset spatula or knife, spread enough of the frosting to cover the layer to the edges. Repeat the same process with the second and third layers. Spread the frosting on the sides of the cake.

Makes 10 cups of frosting.

TIP: This frosting can be made 2 to 3 days ahead. Store any leftover frosting in the refrigerator and rewhip when ready to use.

VANILLA CARAMEL CAKE

This is the cake layer that Aisha Cheeks, one of the decorators at Gabriel's, used in her entry in the competitive cake show Ultimate Cake Off *on the TLC network.*

2¼ cups firmly packed brown sugar
1 cup butter (2 sticks)
1 tablespoon vanilla bean paste
3 eggs
1 teaspoon baking soda

3 cups cake flour
1 teaspoon baking powder
½ cup buttermilk
¼ cup sour cream

Preheat the oven to 350 degrees. Grease and flour three 9-inch round cake pans.

In a medium bowl, using an electric mixer, cream the brown sugar, butter, and vanilla bean paste. Add the eggs one at a time, mixing well after each addition.

Sift the baking soda, cake flour, and baking powder and add to the creamed ingredients just until incorporated. Add the buttermilk, mixing on low speed. Scrape down but do not overmix.

Fold in the sour cream and divide among the prepared pans. Bake for 25 to 30 minutes. The center of the cake will spring back when tapped. Frost with your favorite buttercream or cream cheese frosting.

Makes three 9-inch cake layers.

CHOCOLATE ITALIAN CREAM CAKE

This is the chocolate version of one of our best-selling cakes at Gabriel's Desserts, the Italian Cream Cake featured in Cooking in the South with Johnnie Gabriel. *If you've already experienced the Italian Cream Cake, you'll surely be tempted to try the chocolate one!*

1	stick butter or margarine	2	cups all-purpose flour
1/2	cup vegetable shortening	1	teaspoon baking soda
2	cups sugar	1/4	cup cocoa powder
5	extra-large eggs, separated	1/2	cup coconut, we use Angel Flake
1	cup buttermilk	1	cup pecans
1	teaspoon vanilla extract		

Preheat the oven to 350 degrees. Spray three 9-inch cake pans with nonstick spray.

In a large bowl cream the butter, shortening, and sugar, until well mixed. Add the egg yolks one at a time, beating well after each addition.

In a small bowl combine the buttermilk and vanilla.

In a medium bowl sift together the flour, baking soda, and cocoa. Add to the sugar mixture, alternating with the buttermilk. Begin with 1/4 of the flour mixture (doesn't have to be exact) and blend. Add 1/3 of the buttermilk (again, doesn't need to be exact). End the alternate additions with the flour mixture.* Add the coconut and pecans and gently mix in.

In a smaller bowl whip the egg whites until they form stiff, but not dry peaks. Fold the egg whites into the batter in 2 or 3 additions, being careful not to overmix. Divide the batter evenly into the 3 prepared pans and tap them on the counter surface to level the batter and release any air bubbles. Bake in the oven for 24 to 28 minutes or until the cake tester inserted near the center comes out clean.

Remove the cakes from the oven, set on a wire rack, and cool in the pans for 10 to 15 minutes.

Frost with chocolate cream cheese frosting (page 161). Put your first cake layer on a cake plate and spread $^1/_4$ of the mixture on the first layer. Place the second layer evenly and securely on the top of the frosted layer. Repeat with the third layer. Use remaining frosting to cover the sides of the cake.

Serves 16.

TIP: If any of your layers are significantly higher in the middle of the layer, level the layer with a serrated knife to keep the layers from breaking when they are stacked.

---

* My grandmother taught me in mixing a cake to alternately add the dry ingredients with the liquid ingredients. I make 4 additions of flour and 3 of liquid. It's a good general rule to follow unless the recipe tells you differently.

CHOCOLATE
CREAM CHEESE FROSTING

Delicious on our Chocolate Italian Cream Cake, but don't hesitate to be creative and use this with other favorite recipes.

1 1/2	sticks butter or margarine (6 ounces)	1/4	cup plus 2 tablespoons cocoa powder, divided
12	ounces cream cheese	1 1/2	teaspoons vanilla extract
3	cups confectioners' sugar, sifted		

In a large bowl combine the butter and cream cheese and cream together. In a medium bowl combine the confectioners' sugar and cocoa and sift. Add the sugar mixture in increments to the cream cheese mixture, scraping down the bottom and sides of the bowl once or twice between additions. Add the vanilla and mix well.

Frosts three 9-inch layers or one large pound cake with leftover frosting.

OLD SOUTH SPICE CAKE

When Liz Cole arrived in Evansville, Indiana, a few days before her brother's wedding, he asked if she could make a spice cake to serve as his groom's cake. Excited that he held her in such high esteem as a cook and confident in her ability to get things done, but a bit nervous, she whipped up the following cake. Good spice cake recipes are not that easy to find, so I asked her to share this one with us. According to the guests, she made her brother proud!

Cake:
- 1 cup butter, softened (2 sticks)
- 2 cups sugar
- 5 eggs
- 2 cups all-purpose flour
- 1/2 cup cocoa powder
- 2 teaspoons ground allspice
- 2 teaspoons ground cinnamon
- 1 teaspoon ground cloves
- 1/2 teaspoon salt
- 1 teaspoon baking soda
- 1 cup buttermilk

Nut and fruit filling:
- 1 (14-ounce) can sweetened condensed milk
- 1 1/2 cups sifted confectioners' sugar
- 1 teaspoon ground allspice
- 1 teaspoon ground cinnamon
- 1/4 teaspoon ground cloves
- 1 1/2 cups raisins, chopped lightly in a food processor
- 1 cup chopped pecans

Preheat the oven to 375 degrees. Grease and flour three 9-inch cake pans.

Make the cake: In a large bowl cream the butter. Gradually add the sugar, beating well. Add the eggs, one at a time, beating well after each addition.

In a medium bowl combine the flour, cocoa, allspice, cinnamon, cloves, and salt.

In a small bowl dissolve the baking soda in the buttermilk.

Add the flour mixture to the creamed mixture alternately with the buttermilk mixture, beginning and ending with the flour. Pour the batter into the prepared cake pans and bake for 20 minutes or until a wooden pick inserted in the center comes out clean. Cool in the pans for 10 minutes. Remove the layers from the pans and cool completely on wire racks.

Make the filling: Combine the sweetened condensed milk, confectioners' sugar, allspice, cinnamon, cloves, ground raisins, and chopped pecans. Spread the filling between the cake layers.

Frost the top and sides of the cake with caramel frosting (page 175).

Serves 16 to 18.

TIP: Decorate with pecan halves around the base of the cake. Piped chocolate designs on the caramel frosting, using melted chocolate in a pastry bag, would further dress up the cake for special occasions.

BLUEBERRY COFFEECAKE

This recipe is from Louise Kugler, who works at Gabriel's. She is a great baker, and we are fortunate to include several of her recipes.

Cake:

1¼	cups sugar
3	cups all-purpose flour
3	teaspoons baking powder
¾	teaspoon salt
8	tablespoons butter, cold
2	eggs
¾	cup milk
1	pint blueberries (2 cups)

Topping:

1	cup flour
1	cup sugar
1	tablespoon ground cinnamon
8	tablespoons butter

Make the cake: Preheat the oven to 375 degrees. Grease and flour one 13 x 9-inch pan.

In a large bowl combine the sugar, flour, baking powder, and salt, mixing well. With a pastry blender, cut the butter into the dry ingredients until it resembles coarse crumbs.

Stir the eggs and milk together and add to the dry ingredients, stirring just until moistened. Fold in the blueberries and spread in the prepared pan.

Make the topping: Combine the flour, sugar, and cinnamon in a medium bowl. Cut the butter into the flour mixture until it resembles coarse crumbs.

Spoon the topping evenly over the cake batter. Bake about 45 minutes or until a toothpick inserted in the center comes out clean.

Serves 16 to 18.

TIP: If you don't have a pastry blender, you can use two knives, crisscrossing them in the bowl to literally cut the butter into the flour.

Double-Fudge Chocolate Cupcakes

If you like chocolate and peanut butter you are going to love these cupcakes. For an extra special treat, garnish with peanut butter cup halves and chocolate sprinkles (photo on page 263).

Cake

1 1/2	cups hot, brewed coffee
3	ounces semisweet chocolate
3/4	teaspoon vanilla
3	cups sugar
4	large eggs, at room temperature
3/4	cup vegetable oil
2 1/2	cups sifted all-purpose flour
1 1/2	cups cocoa powder
2	teaspoons baking soda
3/4	teaspoon baking powder
1 1/4	teaspoons salt
1 1/2	cups buttermilk

Peanut Butter Buttercream Frosting:

3	cups Vanilla Buttercream Frosting (see page 156)
1	cup peanut butter

Preheat the oven to 350 degrees.

Make the cupcakes: In a small bowl pour the hot coffee over the semisweet chocolate, stirring with a whisk to evenly melt the chocolate. Whisk in the vanilla. In a large mixing bowl mix the sugar, eggs, and oil. Add the melted chocolate mixture. In another large bowl sift together the flour, cocoa powder, baking soda, baking powder, and salt. Add the flour mixture and the buttermilk alternately in three to four increments to the sugar mixture, beginning with the flour and ending with the flour.

Line two 12-cup muffin pans with cupcake liners and fill each cup 2/3 full. Bake for 20 to 24 minutes, or until the center of cupcakes spring back when touched. Remove from the oven and allow to cool completely in the pans.

Make the frosting: In a medium mixing bowl add the vanilla buttercream frosting and the peanut butter and combine with a hand mixer until well blended.

Makes 24 cupcakes.

RASPBERRY CREAM CHEESE COFFEECAKE

Another delicious Louise Kugler coffeecake.

2 1/4	cups all-purpose flour	2	eggs
1	cup sugar, divided	1	teaspoon almond extract
3/4	cup butter or margarine	1	(8-ounce) package cream cheese, softened
1/2	teaspoon baking powder		
1/2	teaspoon baking soda	1/2	cup raspberry preserves
1/4	teaspoon salt	1/2	cup sliced almonds
3/4	cup sour cream		

Preheat the oven to 350 degrees. Grease and flour the bottom and sides of a 9-inch or 10-inch springform pan.

In a large bowl combine the flour and 3/4 cup of the sugar. Using a pastry blender or fork, cut in the butter or margarine until the mixture resembles coarse crumbs. Set aside 1 cup of the crumb mixture.

To the remaining crumb mixture, add the baking powder, baking soda, salt, sour cream, 1 of the eggs, and the almond extract and blend well. Spread the batter over the bottom and 2 inches up the sides of the prepared pan. Batter should be about 1/4-inch thick on the sides.

In a small bowl combine the cream cheese, the remaining 1/4 cup sugar and the remaining egg, blending well. Pour over the batter in the pan.

Carefully spoon the preserves evenly over the cheese filling.

In a small bowl combine the 1 cup reserved crumb mixture and the sliced almonds. Sprinkle over the top. Bake for 45 to 55 minutes or until the cream cheese filling is set and the crust is deep golden brown. Cool 15 minutes and remove the sides of the pan.

Serve warm or cool; cut into wedges. Refrigerate any leftovers.

Serves 12.

GOOD GRANNY'S POUND CAKE

This recipe is from Jo Ann Hughes's recipe collection. It was her mother's. I hope my grandchildren will one day refer to me as having been a "good granny." Jo Ann is the sister of Gail Schwartz, another good cook whose recipes you will see in Second Helpings. *Gail is one of my Monday night Bible study buddies. Thanks, Jo Ann, for sharing!*

2	sticks butter, room temperature	1	teaspoon lemon extract
1/2	cup vegetable shortening, room temperature	1	teaspoon almond extract
		1	cup skim milk, room temperature
3	cups sugar	3	cups flour, sifted
6	eggs, room temperature		

Do not preheat the oven.

In a large bowl cream the butter, shortening, and sugar, mixing well. Add the eggs one at a time and occasionally scrape down the sides and bottom of the bowl. Mix the lemon and almond extracts with the milk.

In three additions alternately add the flour and milk, beginning and ending with the flour. Beat just until the flour is combined.

Grease and flour a tube pan, not an angel food pan.* Pour the cake batter into the pan, gently leveling the top of the batter with a spatula. Tap the pan several times on the countertop to get any air bubbles out and settle the batter into the pan.

With the oven set at 325 degrees, turn the oven on and place the cake into the cold oven. Bake for approximately 1 hour and 15 minutes until the top cracks.

Serves 14.

---

* Because an angel food pan is made of two pieces, the bottom often doesn't fit securely enough after several washings, which causes the pound cake batter to leak out.

APPLE POUND CAKE

I have seen many apple pound cake recipes, but this one from Evelyn Elliott's collection is somewhat different with the addition of coconut.

Cake:
- 2 cups sugar
- 3 eggs, well beaten
- 1¹/3 cups vegetable oil
- 2 teaspoons vanilla extract
- 3 cups all-purpose sifted flour
- 1 teaspoon ground cinnamon
- 1 teaspoon salt
- 1 teaspoon baking soda
- 3 cups chopped, peeled Granny Smith apples
- 1 cup chopped nuts
- 2 cups coconut, Angel Flake or other processed coconut

Glaze:
- 1 cup firmly packed brown sugar
- 1 stick butter or margarine
- ¹/4 cup milk

Preheat the oven to 325 degrees. Grease and flour a tube pan.

Make the cake: In a large bowl, using an electric mixer, cream the sugar and eggs until fluffy. Add the oil and vanilla and blend well.

In another bowl, sift the flour with the cinnamon, salt, and baking soda and add the mixture to the sugar and oil mixture. Stir in the apples, nuts, and the coconut. Pour into the prepared tube pan and bake for 1¹/2 hours.

Make the glaze: In a medium saucepan over medium heat, combine the brown sugar, butter, and milk, stirring to melt the butter and sugar. Bring to a boil and boil for 2 minutes, making sure the sugar is melted. Pour over the cake while the cake is still warm.

Serves 14 to 16.

NEW ORLEANS
CHERRY DATE NUT CAKE

This recipe has been used in Liz Cole's family for years. It is a delicious variation of a traditional fruitcake, without all the candied citrus fruit. It uses dates and cherries, which most folks like.

2	pounds dates, cut in quarters	1	cup all-purpose flour
4	cups pecan halves	1/2	tablespoon baking powder
1	pound red or green candied cherries, cut in half	1/2	tablespoon salt
		4	eggs
1	cup sugar	2	teaspoons vanilla extract

Preheat the oven to 300 degrees. Line two 9 x 5 x 2 1/2-inch loaf pans with parchment paper.

Place the dates, pecans, and cherries in a large bowl. Sift the sugar, flour, baking powder, and salt over the fruit and nuts. Mix well.

In a small bowl beat the eggs until foamy. Add the vanilla and stir to combine. Add the egg mixture to the fruit mixture. Pour into the 2 prepared loaf pans. With the back of a spatula, press the batter down so no air remains in the pans. Bake for 1 hour. Remove from the oven and let cool on a wire rack in the pans.

Makes 2 loaves.

NOTE: Candied fruit is impossible to find in grocery stores except during Thanksgiving and Christmas holidays. I found it from suppliers on the internet available year round. I ordered from www.nutsonline.com.

KEY LIME MOUSSE CAKE

This is a delicious specialty cake that we make at Gabriel's Desserts in the spring and summer. Lime and white chocolate are two of my favorite flavors—the combination is delightfully refreshing.

Crust:
- 1 cup graham cracker crumbs
- 2 tablespoons firmly packed brown sugar
- 1 stick butter, softened (room temperature)

Mousse filling:
- 3 ounces key lime juice (6 tablespoons plus 1 teaspoon)

- 3 gelatin sheets or 3/4 teaspoon granulated gelatin
- 2 1/2 cups heavy cream, divided
- 9 ounces white chocolate, chopped
- 3 (8-ounce) package cream cheese
- 1 cup sugar
- zest of 2 limes
- sliced fresh strawberries and white chocolate curls or whipped cream and white chocolate curls, for garnish

Preheat the oven to 350 degrees,

Prepare the crust: In a medium bowl combine the graham cracker crumbs and the brown sugar. Mix the butter into the crumb mixture (I use my hands) combining well until all the crumbs are wet. Firmly press the crumbs into the bottom and 1 inch up the sides of a springform pan. Bake 5 to 8 minutes. Remove and set aside to cool until ready to fill.

Make the filling: Place the lime juice and gelatin in a bowl over boiling water and leave until the gelatin is dissolved.

In another saucepan bring 1/2 cup of the heavy cream to a light boil. Add the white chocolate and stir until melted and smooth. Stir in the gelatin mixture and cool slightly.

In a large bowl combine the cream cheese, sugar, and lime zest, and beat until smooth. Slowly add the white chocolate mixture to the cream cheese mixture.

In a medium bowl whip the remaining 2 cups heavy cream into stiff peaks and fold into the cream cheese mixture. Spread the mixture over the cooled graham cracker crust. Level the top with a spatula, and tap lightly on the countertop to settle the mousse. Put in the freezer for 5 to 6 hours until frozen.

Take out of the freezer and remove the ring from the springform pan by running a knife that has been dipped in hot water around the edge to loosen and release the spring on the side of the pan. Invert the frozen mousse, remove the metal bottom, and replace with the serving plate. Return the mousse cake to right side up.

Defrost in the refrigerator for 4 to 6 hours before serving.

To serve: Cut into wedges and garnish with a few slices of fresh strawberries and white chocolate curls or a dollop of fresh whipped cream and white chocolate curls.

Serves 14 to 16.

BEESTING CAKE

An unusual name for a cake for sure. This is one of Susan Johnson's favorite desserts.

Pecan topping:
- 1/2 cup butter, melted
- 1 cup finely chopped pecans
- 1/2 cup sugar
- 2 tablespoons milk
- 2 teaspoons vanilla extract

Cake:
- 1/3 cup sugar
- 1/2 cup butter, softened (1 stick)
- 1 large egg

- 2 cups flour, sifted
- 2 teaspoons baking powder
- 2 tablespoons milk

Buttercream filling:
- 1/4 cup sweet butter, creamed (1/2 stick)
- 1 cup confectioners' sugar plus extra to sprinkle over the cake
- 1 teaspoon vanilla extract
- 1 (10-ounce) jar seedless raspberry jam

Preheat the oven to 400 degrees. Butter one 8-inch springform pan.

Make the topping: In a saucepan combine the butter, pecans, sugar, milk, and vanilla. Bring to a boil, stirring constantly, making sure the sugar melts. Set aside to cool.

Make the cake: In a large bowl blend the sugar, butter, and egg, mixing well. Add the flour, baking powder, and milk and combine well. Pour into the prepared springform pan. Pour the cooled pecan topping on top. Spread evenly. Bake for 25 to 30 minutes. Cool; remove from the pan. Slice in half horizontally.

Make buttercream filling: Combine the butter, confectioners' sugar, and the vanilla. Mix until smooth. Spread one layer with the buttercream filling and the other with the seedless raspberry jam. Reassemble with the two layers facing each other, and sprinkle the cake with confectioners' sugar.

Serves 10 to 12.

TIP: I had not seen an 8-inch springform pan. Susan found hers on the Sur Le Table Web site. I'm sure they can be found at other kitchen stores, for example, Cooks Warehouse in Atlanta, Georgia.

Caramel Frosting

Caramel frosting is a true southern dish, but you sure don't have to be southern to enjoy it!

2	cups sugar	1/2	teaspoon baking soda
1/2	cup firmly packed brown sugar	1	cup buttermilk
1/2	cup butter	2	tablespoons light corn syrup

In a large heavy saucepan, combine the sugar, brown sugar, butter, baking soda, buttermilk, and corn syrup. Cook over medium heat, stirring until the sugar dissolves. Cook until a candy thermometer reaches the soft ball stage (236 degrees).

Cool the mixture slightly. Beat until the mixture reaches spreading consistency. Use while easy to spread.

Makes enough frosting for the top and sides of one 3-layer cake.

TIP: Work rapidly when frosting a cake with this recipe as it sets up quickly.

MOLTEN CHOCOLATE LAVA CAKES

Calling all lovers of chocolate. Well worth the effort!

. . . .

13	ounces semisweet chocolate (about 3 cups, chopped)	9	egg yolks
6	tablespoons unsalted butter (3 ounces)	1/2	cup sugar, divided
		3	egg whites
			pinch of salt

. . . .

Preheat the oven to 400 degrees.

Butter and flour a 12-cup muffin pan or use 10 to 12 individual molds of approximately the same size as a muffin cup.

Chop the chocolate and place in a microwave-proof bowl. Melt in the microwave in 1-minute increments, stirring after each minute, until the chocolate is soft. Add the butter and microwave for 1 additional minute. Stir until the butter is incorporated and set aside to cool slightly.

In a large bowl using a balloon whisk, whip the egg yolks and 6 tablespoons of the sugar (all of the sugar less 2 tablespoons) to a ribbon stage.* Incorporate the chocolate mixture into the egg mixture and set aside.

In another bowl use a balloon whisk to whip the egg whites and a pinch of salt until they are foamy. Add the remaining 2 tablespoons sugar and continue to whisk until the whites form soft peaks. Carefully fold the egg whites into the chocolate mixture. Pour the batter into each of the cups three fourths full. Bake for approximately 8 minutes. Don't overbake. The cake should jiggle in the cup, indicating that the center will be loose—as it should be.

Serves 10 to 12.

* See the glossary for tips to achieve a perfect ribbon stage.

ITALIAN SPRINKLE COOKIES

This is one of the recipes Louise Kugler shared with me from her years spent in New York.

Cookie dough:
- 6 eggs
- 5 cups all-purpose flour
- 2 cups confectioners' sugar
- 2 tablespoons plus 1½ teaspoons baking powder
- 1 cup vegetable oil
- 1 tablespoon almond extract
- 1½ teaspoons lemon extract

Glaze:
- ½ cup warm milk
- 1 teaspoon almond extract
- 1 teaspoon vanilla extract
- 3¾ cups confectioners' sugar colored sprinkles

Preheat the oven to 350 degrees.

Make the cookie dough: In a large bowl beat the eggs until light and foamy, about 5 minutes. Set aside.

In another large bowl combine the flour, sugar, and baking powder. Stir in the oil and almond and lemon extracts. Gradually add the eggs to the flour mixture. The dough will be stiff. Roll the dough into 1-inch balls and place on ungreased baking sheets. Bake for 12 minutes, or until the edges begin to brown.

Make the glaze: In a large bowl combine the milk and the almond and vanilla extracts. Add the confectioners' sugar and whisk until a smooth glaze forms.

As soon as you remove the cookies from the oven, immerse two or three at a time in the glaze. Remove with a slotted spoon and place on wire racks to drip. Quickly sprinkle the tops with colored sprinkles.*

Let the cookies dry for 24 hours. Store in airtight containers.

Makes about 7 dozen.

TIP: If your oven browns unevenly, halfway through the baking time turn the baking sheet.

* At this point it is helpful to have two people working. The sprinkles need to go on the cookies as soon as they come out of the glaze.

CHOCOLATE CHIP OATMEAL COOKIES

We sell dozens of these every day at Gabriel's. A little twist on both the chocolate chunk cookie and the traditional oatmeal.

1	cup butter or margarine	1/2	teaspoon salt
1	cup vegetable oil	1/2	teaspoon cream of tartar
1	cup firmly packed brown sugar	1	cup regular oats, uncooked
1	cup sugar	1	cup rice cereal
1	egg	1	(12-ounce) package semisweet
2	teaspoons vanilla extract		chocolate morsels
3 1/2	cups all-purpose flour	3/4	cup chopped pecans
1	teaspoon baking soda		

Preheat the oven to 375 degrees.

In a large bowl, using an electric mixer, cream the butter and oil, gradually adding the brown sugar and white sugar, blending and beating at medium speed. Add the egg and vanilla, mixing well.

In a medium bowl combine the flour, baking soda, salt, and cream of tartar. Gradually add the dry mixture to the creamed mixture, mixing well. Stir in the oats, rice cereal, chocolate morsels, and chopped pecans. Drop by teaspoonfuls onto greased cookie sheets. Bake for 14 to 16 minutes. Cool on wire racks.

Makes 10 dozen cookies.

TIP: If your cookies spread too thin and don't hold a cookie shape when you bake them, try refrigerating the dough about 30 minutes before baking.

DRIED CRANBERRY BISCOTTI

Start the day right with homemade biscotti and a cup of coffee. A recipe from the collection of Susan Johnson.

1¹/2	cups sugar	2¹/2	cups flour
¹/2	cup unsalted butter, room temperature (1 stick)	1	teaspoon baking powder
		¹/2	teaspoon salt
2	large eggs	1¹/2	cups dried cranberries
¹/2	teaspoon almond extract	1	egg white

Preheat the oven to 350 degrees. Line a large baking sheet with parchment paper.

In a large bowl beat the sugar, butter, eggs, and almond extract until well mixed.

In a medium bowl combine the flour, baking powder, and salt. Add to the butter mixture. Add the dried cranberries. Divide the dough in half. On a floured surface form into one 2¹/2-inch-wide x 9¹/2-inch-long x 1-inch-high log. Transfer to the prepared baking sheet.

In a small bowl whisk the egg white and brush on the top and sides of the log. Bake the log until golden brown, 30 to 35 minutes. Cool completely on the parchment paper on a rack.

Transfer the log to a cutting board. Discard the parchment. Cut the log into ¹/2-inch-wide slices. Arrange the slices on the baking sheet. Bake for 5 to 10 minutes. Turn over and bake an additional 5 minutes. Transfer to wire racks to cool.

Makes about 28 biscotti.

Jam Squares

This recipe was given to Liz Cole by Mike Albrecht, a former student of hers at Dickerson Middle School, when he was in the sixth grade. He made the Jam Squares for his math class when they studied fractions, and she makes them for our Sunday school class. Mike's father is chef Paul Albrecht, whose tenure with the Buckhead Life Group restaurants, including Pano's and Paul's and Atlanta Fish Market, contributed to the development of Atlanta's culinary identity. Chef Paul can be found at his Midtown restaurant, Spice.

2	cups plus 1 tablespoon all-purpose flour	1	egg
1/4	teaspoon salt	1	teaspoon vanilla extract
3/4	cup butter	1	(16-ounce) jar strawberry preserves, or your favorite preserves
1	cup sugar		

Preheat the oven to 350 degrees.

In a small bowl mix the flour and the salt.

In a large bowl add the butter and sugar; mix until well combined. Add the egg, the flour mixture, and the vanilla, mixing just until ingredients are combined. Press 3/4 of the mixture over the bottom of a 13 x 9-inch pan. Spread the preserves over the batter.

Pinching off pieces of the remaining flour mixture, scatter over the top of the preserves. Both the batter and the preserves are visible on top.

Bake for 25 to 30 minutes until the top is light brown. Cool and cut into squares.

Makes 32 to 36 jam squares.

Tip: To make your clean up a cinch, spray the pan with a pan-coating mixture or line the pan with parchment paper.

A great little holiday cookie from Evelyn Elliott. Perfect for anyone who likes the candied fruit at Christmas but doesn't want a whole piece of fruitcake.

1/2	cup sugar	1	pound dates, chopped**
1/3	cup butter or margarine	1	pound chopped pecans
2	eggs, well beaten		(we use 6 cups)
1 1/2	cups all-purpose flour	1	pound candied pineapple,
1 1/2	teaspoons baking soda		chopped
1 1/2	tablespoons milk	3/4	cup red grape juice
1	pound candied cherries, chopped*		

Preheat the oven to 325 degrees.

In a large bowl cream the sugar, butter, and eggs.

In medium bowl sift together the flour and baking soda and add to the creamed mixture. Stir in the milk and then add the chopped cherries, dates, pecans, pineapple and grape juice. Drop by teaspoonfuls on a greased cookie sheet, and bake for 12 to 15 minutes.

Makes 100 cookies.

TIP: These make great gifts. Packed in a tin, they will keep a couple of weeks.

* In years past I have tried to use a food processor to chop the fruit, but even just pulsing left the fruit gooey. Flouring a sharp knife and chopping by hand worked best for me.

** You can buy chopped dates—a great time saver.

LEMON SAUCER COOKIES

Lemon is such a refreshing flavor. Susan Johnson highly recommends these cookies.

Cookies:
- 1/2 cup unsalted butter, softened (1 stick)
- 1/2 cup vegetable oil
- 1/2 cup granulated sugar
- 1/2 cup confectioners' sugar
- 1 large egg
- 1 teaspoon vanilla extract
- 1 teaspoon lemon extract
- zest of one lemon
- 2 cups all-purpose flour, sifted
- 1 1/2 teaspoons baking soda
- 1/4 teaspoon salt

Frosting:
- 1 cup confectioners' sugar, sifted
- juice of 1 lemon

Make the cookies: In the bowl of an electric mixer, beat the butter for 1 minute. Add the following ingredients one at a time: the oil, granulated sugar, confectioners' sugar, egg, vanilla and lemon extracts, and the lemon zest. Beat well after adding each ingredient.

In a medium bowl combine the flour, baking soda, and salt, and stir into the butter/sugar mixture all at once. Refrigerate the dough for 1 hour or overnight.

Preheat the oven to 350 degrees and line the cookie sheet(s) with parchment paper. Form balls with 1 tablespoon each of the dough and place on the parchment. Make a well in the center of each ball by depressing slightly in the center. Bake for 8 to 10 minutes, until lightly browned on the edges.

Make the frosting: While the cookies are baking, combine the confectioners' sugar with the lemon juice.

Cool the cookies briefly on a wire rack. While the cookies are still slightly warm, spoon the frosting over the cookies. Let dry 20 to 30 minutes.

Makes 2 dozen cookies.

MOCHA-FROSTED CHOCOLATE CHIP COOKIES

Chocolate and coffee team up in another taste treat from Susan Johnson's collection.

Cookies:
- 1 cup all-purpose flour
- 3 tablespoons cocoa powder
- 1 teaspoon baking soda
- 1/4 teaspoon salt
- 1 stick butter
- 2/3 cup firmly packed golden brown sugar
- 1/4 cup granulated sugar
- 1 large egg
- 2 teaspoons water
- 1 teaspoon instant coffee
- 1 teaspoon vanilla extract
- 2 cups chocolate chips
- 1 cup coarsely chopped nuts

Mocha frosting:
- 1/2 cup semisweet chocolate chips
- 1/2 cup whipping cream
- 1 tablespoon instant coffee
- 6 tablespoons butter, softened
- 1 1/2 teaspoon vanilla extract
- 1 cup confectioners' sugar

Preheat the oven to 325 degrees.

Make the cookies: In a medium bowl combine the flour, cocoa, baking soda, and salt and set aside.

In a large bowl beat the butter, brown sugar, and granulated sugar until well blended. Add the egg, water, instant coffee, vanilla, chocolate chips, and nuts and blend well, but do not beat. Add the flour mixture and combine.

Line a cookie sheet with parchment paper. Drop dough by tablespoons 2 inches apart onto the lined cookie sheet. Bake for 13 minutes until firm and no longer shiny. Cool on the sheets for 10 minutes.

Make the frosting: In a medium microwavable bowl, melt the chocolate chips in the microwave in 1-minute intervals, stirring after each minute until the chocolate is soft.

In a small bowl mix together the whipping cream and the instant coffee and add to the chocolate mixture. Using an electric mixer add the butter, vanilla, and confectioners' sugar. Frost the cookies. Store cookies in the refrigerator.

Makes 4 dozen cookies.

LEMON ICE CREAM PIE

Trish Elliott contributed this recipe. The sweet ice cream and the tart lemon backed up with a salty crust. Yum!

Crust:
- 1¹/2 cups crushed pretzels
- ¹/4 cup sugar
- ¹/2 cup butter or margarine

Filling:
- 1 quart vanilla ice cream, slightly thawed
- 1 small can frozen lemonade, thawed

Fresh raspberries or sliced strawberries for garnish

Preheat the oven to 350 degrees.

In a medium bowl combine the pretzels, sugar, and butter. Firmly press into the bottom of a 9-inch pie plate. Bake in the oven for 5 to 6 minutes, just to set the crust.

In a medium bowl combine the ice cream and lemonade, blending well. Spread over the pretzel crust and freeze.

Let thaw 5 minutes before serving. Garnish with fresh raspberries or sliced strawberries.

Serves 8.

VARIATION: For a change use a small can of frozen limeade.

WHOOPIE PIES

Mo Bednarowski, our front of the house manager, gave me her grandmother's (Estelle Dube) recipe for Whoopie Pies. Mo grew up in Massachusetts where they had the pleasure of eating homemade ones. I guess they're the equivalent of the south's moon pie, except much better and homemade!

Cake:
- 1 cup shortening
- 2 cups sugar
- 2 eggs
- 2 cups milk
- 2 teaspoons vanilla extract
- 4 cups all-purpose flour
- 1 teaspoon salt
- 1 cup cocoa powder
- 3 teaspoons baking soda
- 1 teaspoon baking powder

Filling:
- 1 cup shortening
- 2 cups marshmallow creme
- 2 cups confectioners' sugar
- 2 to 4 tablespoons milk
- 2 teaspoons vanilla

Make the cakes: Preheat the oven to 400 degrees. In a large bowl cream the shortening and sugar. Add the eggs, milk, and vanilla and mix well. Scrape down the bottom and side of the bowl.

In another large bowl sift the flour, salt, cocoa, baking soda, and baking powder and add to the egg and sugar mixture, blending well.

On a parchment-lined baking sheet, place heaping tablespoons of batter, 2 inches apart. Bake for 10 minutes. Remove from the oven to cool while you prepare the filling.

Make the filling: In a large bowl cream the shortening and marshmallow. Add the confectioners' sugar, milk, and vanilla. Beat for 3 minutes.

Assemble the pies: Turn half of the chocolate pies flat side up. Using a heaping tablespoon, place a scoop of the marshmallow creme on top of each pie. Place the other half of the pies flat side down over the marshmallow creme, to form a sandwich.

Makes 3 dozen pies.

TIP: Melt 1/2 cup semisweet chocolate chips with 2 teaspoons of shortening and drizzle in a crisscross pattern over the top of the pies.

PUMPKIN WHOOPIE PIES

Mo Bednarowski grew up eating her grandmother's chocolate whoopie pies. As a pastry chef, she developed her own recipe for pumpkin whoopie pies. These are delicious!

Cake:
- 3 cups all-purpose flour
- 2 tablespoons ground cinnamon
- 2 teaspoons baking powder
- 1 1/2 teaspoons ground nutmeg
- 1 1/2 teaspoons ground ginger
- 1 teaspoon baking soda
- 1 teaspoon salt
- 1/2 teaspoon ground cloves
- 1 1/4 cups butter
- 1 1/2 cups sugar
- 3 tablespoons molasses

- 2 teaspoons vanilla extract
- 4 eggs
- 1 (15-ounce) can pumpkin
- 1/2 cup buttermilk

Filling:
- 1 cup shortening
- 2 cups marshmallow creme
- 2 cups confectioner's sugar
- 2 tablespoons milk
- 2 teaspoons vanilla extract

Preheat the oven to 350 degrees.

Make the cakes: In a large bowl sift the flour, cinnamon, baking powder, nutmeg, ginger, baking soda, salt, and cloves, and set aside.

In a large bowl beat the butter, sugar, molasses, and vanilla. Add the eggs slowly and then the pumpkin.

Alternately add the dry mixture and the buttermilk into the egg and sugar mixture in 3 additions. Scrape the bowl down.

Using a heaping tablespoon, scoop the mixture onto a parchment-lined cookie sheet, spacing the scoops 2 inches apart. Bake for 12 to 15 minutes and cool.

Make the filling: In a large bowl cream the shortening and marshmallow creme. Add the confectioner's sugar, milk, and vanilla, beating about 3 minutes.

Turn half of the pies flat side up and using a heaping tablespoon, place the filling on top of the pie and place another pie flat side down on the creme, forming a sandwich.

Makes 3 dozen pies.

STRAWBERRY LAYER CRÈME PIE

You just can't have too many recipes for strawberry dishes. Here's a good one from Mary Miltiades of Magnolia Moments Catering.

Crust:
- 3 cups graham cracker crumbs
- 2 tablespoons sugar
- 1 stick butter, melted

Filling:
- 2 (3.4-ounce) packages French vanilla instant pudding
- 1/2 cup milk
- 16 ounces sour cream
- 1 tablespoon lemon juice
- 24 ounces whipped topping, divided
- 1 quart strawberries, washed and sliced

Make the crust: In a medium bowl combine the graham cracker crumbs, sugar, and melted butter. Press into the bottom of one 13 x 9-inch pan.

Make the filling: In a large bowl combine the pudding, milk, sour cream, lemon juice, and 12 ounces of the whipped topping. Beat until blended.

Assemble the pie: Spoon the pudding mixture over the graham cracker crust. Layer with the sliced strawberries. Top with the remaining 12 ounces whipped topping and refrigerate 4 to 6 hours.

Serves 8.

TIP: Mary says you can use light sour cream, 1% milk, lite whipped topping, and sugar-free instant pudding to make this dessert even lighter.

FROZEN RASPBERRY PIE

Alexis Edwards Amaden, the innkeeper at the Whitlock Inn, gave me this recipe. We made it for the photo shoot and could hardly wait to eat it! It is beautiful and delicious.

1   (10-ounce) package frozen
    raspberries, partially thawed
2   egg whites*
1   cup plus 1 tablespoon sugar
1   tablespoon lemon juice
2   teaspoons almond extract
1   cup whipping cream
1   teaspoon vanilla extract

1   tablespoon Framboise (optional)
1/4 cup sliced, buttered, and toasted
    almonds, chilled
2   (9-inch) prebaked deep-dish
    pie shells, baked according to
    manufacturer's directions, or 2
    baked homemade pie shells

In a large bowl combine the thawed berries, egg whites, 1 cup of the sugar, the lemon juice, and the almond extract and beat at high speed for 15 minutes. During this time, scrape down the sides with a spatula. The volume of the mixture will increase greatly.

In a medium bowl whip the cream with the remaining 1 tablespoon sugar, the vanilla, and the Framboise. If not using the liqueur, add another splash of almond extract. Fold the almonds and whipping cream into the raspberry mixture. Spoon the mixture into the pie shells and freeze.

Remove from the freezer 30 minutes before serving.

Makes two 9-inch pies.

* This is a raw egg product, and even though it will be frozen, if you are concerned with eating a raw egg, you might want to use a pasteurized egg product. The advice from the American Egg Board: The risk is greater for those who are pregnant, elderly, or very young and those with medical problems that have impaired their immune systems. They should avoid any raw and undercooked animal foods.

CARAMEL PECAN APPLE PIE

We have made this apple pie at Gabriel's for years. We added the woven lattice crust, pecans, and the caramel for an extra touch.

2   9-inch deep-dish purchased or
    homemade piecrusts
1/2 cup plus 2 teaspoons granulated
    sugar
5 to 6 cups peeled and sliced Granny
    Smith apples (1/8- to 1/4-inch thick)
1   tablespoon lemon juice
1/2 cup firmly packed brown sugar

2   tablespoons all-purpose flour
2   tablespoons cornstarch
1/2 teaspoon ground cinnamon
1/4 teaspoon ground nutmeg
2   tablespoons butter or margarine,
    cut into pieces
    caramel sauce
1/2 to 3/4 cup pecan pieces

Preheat the oven to 425 degrees.

Place 1 piecrust in a 9-inch pie pan, pressing the crust to fit down in the pan, leaving a 1-inch overhang around the edge. Wet a pastry brush with water and brush the bottom crust to lightly dampen the crust. Sprinkle 2 teaspoons of the sugar around the bottom and sides of the crust.

In a large bowl combine the apples and the lemon juice and stir to cover the apples.

In a small bowl combine the remaining 1/2 cup granulated sugar, brown sugar, flour, cornstarch, cinnamon, and nutmeg, mixing well. Spoon the sugar mixture over the apples, tossing gently to disperse throughout the slices. Place the apples evenly on top of the crust, and drop pieces of the butter evenly over the slices.

Make the woven lattice crust: Lay the remaining piecrust out flat on a lightly floured cloth or countertop. Cut the crust into 1/2-inch strips. They will be a variety of lengths if you are using a purchased round crust. If you have a homemade piecrust, roll out the pastry and cut ten to fourteen 1/2-inch-wide strips.

Moisten the edge of the crust already in the pie pan. Using half of the cut strips, place them across the pie in one direction leaving 1/2 inch between the strips. Fold back, almost to the edge of the pie plate, every other strip, and lay another strip down going in the opposite direction. Unfold the strips you folded back, and then fold back the other strips almost to the edge. Lay another strip parallel and $1/2$ inch away from the strip you just laid, going perpendicular to the original strips. Repeat this process of alternately folding and unfolding, laying perpendicular strips until you have woven a lattice piecrust.

Trim both the top and bottom crust to the edge of the pie plate. Moisten the tines of a fork and press the edges all around the pie to seal the top and bottom together.

Using the thumb and forefinger (pointer) of one hand and the forefinger on the other hand, flute the edge of the pie. Holding your thumb and forefinger about $1/4$ inch apart as though you were going to pinch something, grasp the edge of the piecrust with fingers pointing away from the pie, and with the forefinger on the other hand, press the piecrust in between your thumb and forefinger, forming a fluted edge.

Place the pie on a baking sheet to catch any drips, and bake at 425 degrees for 10 minutes. Reduce the heat to 350 degrees, baking an additional 35 to 40 minutes.

Check at 30 minutes into baking to see if the edges are browning too much. If so, cut strips of aluminum foil and cover all around the edge of the pie to prevent burning. The pie will be golden on top and juices bubbling when done.

Remove from the oven and let cool 10 minutes. Drizzle the desired amount of caramel over the top of the pie and sprinkle pecans to your taste.

Serves 8 to 10.

CHOCOLATE MERINGUE PIE

A recipe from the collection of Evelyn Elliott.

Meringue shell:
- 2 egg whites
- pinch of salt
- 1/8 teaspoon cream of tartar
- 1/2 cup sugar
- 3/4 cup finely chopped pecans or walnuts
- 1/4 teaspoon vanilla extract

Filling:
- 5 ounces Hershey's milk chocolate (1/2 bar)
- 3 tablespoons water
- 1 cup heavy cream, whipped
- 1 tablespoon sugar
- 1/2 teaspoon vanilla extract

Preheat the oven to 300 degrees.

Make the meringue shell: Beat the egg whites and salt until they begin to foam. Add the cream of tartar. When the whites begin to stiffen, add the sugar and beat until stiff. Fold in the nuts and vanilla. Spread over the bottom and up the sides of a greased 9-inch pie pan and bake for 55 minutes. Let cool.

Make the filling: In the top of a double boiler over simmering water, combine the milk chocolate and water, stirring until well blended. Remove from the heat and let cool.

Fold the chocolate into the whipped cream. Add the sugar and vanilla, stir, and spread over the meringue shell. Chill until ready to serve.

Serves 8.

VARIATION: Add 1/2 cup of chopped and toasted almonds to the filling.

FRESH BLUEBERRY CREAM PIE

A delicious pie recipe from Mary Gillis. Blueberries, butter, pecans, and ice cream—how much better can you get, unless you can find a way to add chocolate?

Topping:
- 3 tablespoons cold butter
- 3 tablespoons flour
- 3 tablespoons sugar
- 3 tablespoons chopped pecans

Filling:
- 2 1/2 cups fresh blueberries
- 1 1/4 cups sugar, divided
- 1 cup sour cream
- 2 tablespoons flour
- 1 teaspoon vanilla extract
- 1/4 teaspoon salt
- 1 9-inch unbaked pie shell
  vanilla ice cream, optional

Preheat the oven to 350 degrees.

Make the topping: In a small bowl cut together the butter, flour, sugar, and pecans with a pastry blender or two knives and set aside.

Make the filling: In a medium bowl toss the blueberries with 1/4 cup of the sugar.

In a large bowl mix the remaining sugar, sour cream, flour, vanilla, and salt. Carefully fold in the blueberries. Pour the mixture into the unbaked pie shell and bake for 35 minutes.

Remove the pie from the oven and sprinkle with the topping. Return to the oven and bake 10 minutes longer. Chill pie before serving. Serve with vanilla ice cream if desired.

Serves 8 to 10.

Lemon Meringue Pie

Another Elliott family recipe featuring meringue, this time topping the dessert.

Filling:
- 1¹/2 cups sugar
- ¹/4 cup cornstarch
- 3 tablespoons all-purpose flour
- ¹/4 teaspoon salt
- 4 large eggs, separated (whites used for the meringue)
- 1¹/2 cups water
- ¹/2 cup lemon juice
- ¹/4 teaspoon grated lemon zest (peel)
- 2 tablespoons butter or margarine
- 1 (10-inch) deep-dish pie shell, homemade or purchased, baked according to directions

Meringue:
- 4 large egg whites
- ¹/4 teaspoon cream of tartar
- 6 tablespoons sugar

Heat the oven to 350 degrees.

Make the filling: In the top of a double boiler, combine the sugar, cornstarch, flour, and salt.

In a medium bowl beat the egg yolks until lemon colored. Add the yolks and water to the sugar mixture in the top of the double boiler. Cook, stirring constantly until the mixture begins to thicken. Add the lemon juice and zest and cook 3 minutes longer or until it thickens again. Remove from the heat and add the butter, stirring until melted. Pour into the pie shell and cover with plastic wrap.

Make the meringue: In a small, deep bowl combine the egg whites and cream of tartar and beat at medium speed until they form soft peaks. Add sugar 1 tablespoon at a time, continuing to beat the meringue to form stiff, glossy peaks and until the sugar is dissolved.

Remove the plastic wrap from the filling and spoon the meringue first around the outside edge of the pie, spreading over the edges to seal the meringue to the edge of the crust. Fill the center and using a spatula, dip into the meringue and lift up and out, forming peaks all over the meringue, making sure the edges stay sealed. Place the pie in the oven, baking until the crust is a light golden brown. Check at 15 minutes for browning, and bake no more than 20 minutes.

Cool on a wire rack. Store any leftovers in the refrigerator.

Serves 8.

FRENCH SILK PIE

This is one of my favorite pies from Gabriel's. Everything but the whipped cream is chocolate. My kind of dessert!

Chocolate cookie crumb crust:
- 2 cups chocolate wafer crumbs
- 1/4 cup butter or margarine, melted

Filling:
- 3 ounces unsweetened chocolate, cut into pieces
- 1 cup butter, softened (don't use margarine)

- 1 cup sugar
- 1/2 teaspoon vanilla extract
- 4 eggs

Topping:
- 1 cup whipping cream
- 1/4 to 1/3 cup confectioners' sugar chocolate curls for garnish

Preheat the oven to 350 degrees.

Make the crust: Pulse the chocolate wafers in a food processor until they are crumbs. Add the melted butter and pulse a few more times until combined. Press into the bottom and up the sides of a 9-inch deep-dish pie pan. Bake for 10 minutes. Remove from the oven and allow to cool completely before using.

Make the filling: Melt the chocolate in a double boiler over low heat and set aside to cool.

In a small bowl beat the butter until fluffy. Gradually add the sugar, beating until light and fluffy. Add the cooled chocolate and the vanilla and blend well. Add the eggs, one at a time, beating at high speed for 1 minute after each addition. Beat until the mixture is smooth and fluffy. Pour into the cooled baked shell. Refrigerate at least 2 hours before serving.

Make the topping: In a small bowl beat the whipping cream until foamy, and gradually add the confectioners' sugar, beating until stiff peaks form.

Top the chilled pie with the whipped topping and chocolate curls.

Serves 10.

TIP: If you can't find chocolate wafer crumbs, use Oreos with the filling removed.

CARAMEL PANNA COTTA

Chef Jeff Brister of the Whitlock Inn graciously contributed this recipe for your enjoyment.

1	cup milk	1/2	teaspoon vanilla extract
1	tablespoon unflavored powdered gelatin	1/2	cup (purchased) caramel sauce plus more for garnish
2	cups heavy cream		caramel corn for garnish
1/2	cup sugar		(optional)

Spray six 1-cup souffle cups or teacups with nonstick spray.

Pour the milk into a bowl and sprinkle the gelatin over.

In a small saucepan bring the cream and the sugar to a boil. Slowly ladle the milk in while constantly stirring. Bring the mixture back to a boil and take the mixture off the stove. Stir in the vanilla and caramel, and strain into prepared souffle cups. Chill and refrigerate overnight.

Garnish with more caramel or a caramel corn.

Serves 6.

LIZ'S BREAD PUDDING

This recipe is from Mary Mahoney's Old French House Restaurant in Biloxi, Mississippi. Liz Cole grew up in Biloxi and has fond memories of eating there on very special occasions.

Pudding:
- 6 slices day-old white bread
- 1 teaspoon ground cinnamon
- 1/2 cup seedless raisins
- 2 tablespoons butter, melted
- 4 eggs
- 2 tablespoons plus 1/2 cup sugar
- 2 cups milk
- 1 teaspoon vanilla extract

Rum sauce:
- 2 cups milk
- 1/2 stick butter
- 1/2 cup sugar
- 2 tablespoons all-purpose flour
- 1 tablespoon canola oil
- 1 tablespoon nutmeg
- 1 tablespoon vanilla extract
- Rum to taste

Preheat the oven to 350 degrees.

Make the pudding: Break the bread into small pieces in a 1 1/2-quart baking dish. Sprinkle the cinnamon over the bread and add the raisins and melted butter. Toast the bread mixture lightly in the oven.

In a medium bowl combine the eggs, sugar, milk and vanilla, mixing well. Pour over the bread and bake about 30 minutes or until solid.

Make the sauce: In a medium saucepan over medium heat, combine the milk, butter, and sugar, whisking lightly and bringing to a boil.

While the milk mixture is heating, in a small bowl combine the flour and oil,* mixing until smooth. When the milk mixture comes to a boil, gradually whisk in the flour mixture to thicken the sauce. Remove from the heat and add the nutmeg, vanilla, and rum to taste.

Serve hot over hot pudding.

Serves 8.

* In true Cajun cooking this would be the start of a roux, but the dark color is not necessary for this dish.

Old-Fashioned
Three-Layer Peach Pie

Evelyn Elliott has been cooking for eighty years, and folks just know her dishes are going to be good. Evelyn gave me a recipe for a peach custard pie, and I had one from a cousin, so I combined the two—hope you love it as much as I do.

Fruit layer (bottom):
- 1 purchased piecrust
- 1 (6-ounce) package dried peaches or apples
- 1 cup sugar
- 2 extra-large eggs, separated (whites will be used in the meringue*)
- 1 cup milk
- 1 tablespoon vanilla extract

Custard layer (middle):
- 1/2 cup sugar
- 3 tablespoons all-purpose flour
- 2 extra-large eggs, separated (whites will be used in the meringue)
- 1 cup milk

Meringue layer (top):*
- 4 extra-large egg whites
- 1/2 teaspoon cream of tartar
- 1/4 teaspoon salt
- 1 teaspoon vanilla extract
- 1/2 cup sugar

Preheat the oven to 350 degrees. Place and fit the unbaked piecrust in a 9-inch deep-dish pie pan.

Make the fruit layer (bottom): In a small saucepan over low heat, cook the peaches with enough water to cover. Cook until tender. Drain the peaches in a colander and press out any remaining water. Return the peaches to the saucepan and add the sugar, 2 egg yolks, milk, and vanilla. Turn on low heat and mash the peaches (I used a potato masher, or use an immersion blender) combining all the ingredients. Cook and stir the peaches just long enough to bring them to a light boil. Remove from the heat, pour over the unbaked piecrust, and level the filling.

Bake in the oven for 20 to 25 minutes. The filling will not be totally set. The crust should be golden brown, but if it starts to brown too much, cover the edges with foil.

Make the custard: In a small saucepan combine the sugar and the flour, whisking to mix well. Add the egg yolks and milk and continue whisking. Cook and whisk constantly over low heat until a thick custard forms. The custard will coat the back of a spoon when ready.

Make the meringue: In a mixing bowl, using an electric mixer, whip the egg whites with the cream of tartar until the whites are foamy. Add the salt, vanilla, and sugar (one tablespoon at a time) until the whites form and can hold a stiff peak. With a spatula spread the meringue over the custard, sealing the meringue to the edges of the crust. With the back of a spatula, create peaks in the meringue. Bake in the oven for 20 to 25 minutes.

Let cool at room temperature for 30 minutes and refrigerate for 3 hours before serving. Refrigerate any leftovers.

Serves 8 to 10.

NOTE: I use a spatula to be sure no flour accumulates in the bottom edges of the pot, and a whisk to break up any clumps of flour.

TIP: I use extra-large eggs at home, and that is what I used when I tested this pie. The size of eggs is very important when you are making a custard and meringue. In the fruit and custard parts of the pie, the purpose of the yolk is to thicken, and in the meringue the amount of the egg white is necessary to give volume to create a pretty meringue.

---

* I tried several meringue recipes while doing this book, as well as doing many meringues at Gabriel's. I like Evelyn's recipe for this meringue as well as any I have tried. It whips up beautifully and holds well. All meringues lose some volume after cooling and cutting. The droop-proof ones I tried tasted starchy or didn't work.

PEANUT BUTTER MOUSSE PIE

We serve this pie at Gabriel's Desserts.

1   (9-inch) deep-dish pie shell

Ganache:
3   ounces semisweet chocolate,
    finely chopped
1/2 cup heavy cream

Filling:
2   cups creamy peanut butter
1   cup confectioners' sugar

51/2 cups frozen whipped topping,
    thawed (approximately 1
    (16-ounce) container)

Topping:
1/4 cup Hershey's syrup or extra
    ganache
1/4 cup chopped unsalted peanuts

Prebake the pie shell according to the manufacturer's directions, or if homemade, bake blind.*

Make the ganache: Place the chocolate in a small heatproof bowl.

In a small saucepan bring the heavy cream to slightly boiling and pour over the chocolate. Let stand 5 minutes and then whisk to thoroughly mix. Pour half of the ganache into the bottom of the blind-baked pie shell and set aside the shell to cool.

Make the filling: In a medium bowl, using an electric mixer, beat the peanut butter and the confectioners' sugar together. Fold in the thawed whipped topping.

To assemble the pie: Spread half of the filling over the cooled ganache in the pie shell. Pour the remaining ganache on the peanut butter filling, and with a metal spatula or knife, swirl the ganache into the filling. If the ganache has cooled and is not pourable, reheat the bowl in the microwave in 10-second blasts, stirring in between.

Top with the remaining half of the peanut butter mixture, swirling and forming decorative peaks with the spatula. If you have a large pastry piping bag and a large star tip, you can pipe the remaining filling in a decorative pattern. Drizzle the chocolate syrup over the top of the pie, and sprinkle with the peanuts. If you don't want to purchase chocolate syrup or don't keep any on hand, make an extra half batch of chocolate ganache and save a portion to drizzle on top.

Refrigerate at least 2 hours before serving. Keep any leftovers refrigerated.

Makes 1 pie.

VARIATION: This pie would also be delicious with the chocolate cookie crust recipe on page 201.

---

* *bake blind* simply means baking the pie shell before it is filled. Most purchased pie shells include directions for a blind-baked crust. Simply prick holes all over the bottom of the raw crust to prevent it from rising up off the pie plate while baking. Line the shell with foil or parchment, and fill with dried beans, rice, or pie weights. Pie weights are available either online or where you purchase other baking utensils and are manufactured specifically for this purpose, but dried beans or rice work just as well. You can use the beans many times before discarding. Bake the pie at the recommended temperature according to the recipe or directions. Remove the beans or weights a few minutes before the shell finishes baking to let the crust brown.

PECAN TASSIES

In 2009 Jane Anne and Rick Countryman's son, Taylor, married the lady of his dreams. At the reception he also wanted to include one of the ladies of his past—his maternal grandmother, Sara Jacobs. Gabriel's not only made the wedding cake for Melissa, his bride, but baked pecan tassies to be served at the reception, using his grandmother's recipe. Thankfully, Jane Anne gave us permission to bake them for customers and to publish the recipe here for you.

Pastry dough:
- 1   stick butter, softened
- 1   (3-ounce) package cream cheese, softened
- 1   cup all-purpose flour

Filling:
- 3/4   cup brown sugar
- 2   tablespoons butter
- 1   teaspoon vanilla
- 1   egg
- 2/3   cup chopped pecans

Make the pastry dough: In a medium bowl use an electric mixer to combine the butter and cream cheese. Add the flour and mix until smooth. Place the dough in the refrigerator until firm, about 30 minutes.

Preheat the oven to 350 degrees.

Remove the pastry dough from the refrigerator and roll it into 24 balls. Press and flatten into ungreased mini-muffin tins. Be careful to not make the bottom of the shell too thin. If it breaks, the filling will seep out and stick to the pan.

Make the filling: In a medium bowl combine the brown sugar, butter, vanilla, and egg, mixing well. Add the pecans and fill the pastry shells.

Bake 30 minutes. Cool before removing from the tins.

Makes 20 to 24 tassies.

MAMMY'S BANANA PUDDING

This recipe is a gift from my friend Elisha Inman Shamblin. Like me, Elisha has wonderful memories of her grandmother's cooking. Mammy lived with Elisha, her mother, and two brothers to help with the cooking, cleaning, and laundry while her mother worked. The food was not fancy, but it was delicious. When Mammy made banana pudding, Elisha would hover, just waiting to lick the pan.

2	cups whole milk	2	tablespoons cornstarch
2	eggs, separated	1	teaspoon vanilla extract
2/3	cup plus 1/4 cup sugar, divided	1	box vanilla wafers
1/8	teaspoon salt	3	bananas, not green or overly ripe

Preheat the oven to 425 degrees.

Scald (see glossary) the milk in the top of a double boiler over boiling water.

Meanwhile in a small bowl, beat the egg yolks. Add 2/3 cup of the sugar, the salt, and the cornstarch to the egg yolks. (Reserve the egg whites for the meringue.) When the milk is just about to boil, remove the top of the double boiler from the heat. Pour 1/2 cup of the milk into the eggs to temper (see glossary) the mixture, stirring constantly to blend.

Return the egg and milk mixture to the top of the double boiler and continue to cook and stir over the boiling water until the mixture is smooth and thickened, about 6 minutes. The custard is ready when it coats the back of a spoon.

Remove from the heat and add the vanilla.

In a 9-inch square x 2-inch deep baking dish, arrange a layer of vanilla wafers to cover the bottom and sides of the dish. Thinly slice all the bananas in a layer over the vanilla wafers. You will have leftover vanilla wafers. Pour the hot custard over the bananas and allow to cool.

In a medium bowl beat the egg whites, gradually adding the remaining 1/4 cup sugar. Beat until the whites are stiff and glossy, but not dry. With a spatula spread the egg whites over the pudding mixture, sealing the whites to the edge of the dish.

Bake for 15 minutes or until the meringue is golden brown.

Serves 6 to 8.

Sweet Potato Bread Pudding

Another delicious bread pudding from Jessica Jacobs. We served this at a March of Dimes benefit, and it was the most requested of all desserts served that night. Time-consuming but worth it

Bread pudding:

- 3 sweet potatoes, peeled and diced
- 1 stick butter, melted, plus extra for buttering parchment
- 3/4 cup firmly packed brown sugar plus a handful
- 4 eggs
- 6 egg yolks
- 1 quart heavy cream
- 1 cup orange juice
- 1 can sweetened condensed milk
- 1/2 cup molasses
- 2 teaspoons ground nutmeg
- 3/4 teaspoon ground ginger
- 1 teaspoon salt
- 2 teaspoons ground cinnamon
- 1/2 cup golden raisins
- 12 brioche rolls or 1 1/2 loaves, diced

Whiskey sauce:

- 1 1/2 cups sugar
- 1/4 cup water
- 1/3 cup butter, cubed
- 3/4 cup heavy cream
- 1/2 cup whiskey
- 1/4 teaspoon salt

Sweet and Salty Roasted Pecans (page 36), for garnish

Preheat the oven to 350 degrees.

Make the bread pudding: Peel and dice the sweet potatoes.

In a large bowl mix the butter, diced potatoes, and the handful of brown sugar. Mix with your hands, covering the potatoes with the mixture as well as you can. Spread the potatoes and any butter and sugar out on a cookie sheet lined with parchment paper (may take more than one sheet). Place in the oven 15 to 20 minutes to caramelize.

Turn the oven temperature down to 300 degrees and remove the potatoes to cool.

In a large bowl whisk the eggs and yolks, cream, orange juice, condensed milk, the remaining 3/4 cup brown sugar, the molasses, nutmeg, ginger, salt, cinnamon, and raisins. Add the bread. Let stand about 15 minutes to absorb the egg mixture.

Spray and line one 13 x 9-inch pan with parchment paper and spread butter liberally on the paper. Carefully pour the sweet potatoes into the egg mixture and gently mix well, being careful not to mash the potatoes. Place in the oven in a water bath. Bake about 1 hour. The middle should be firm. If the pudding browns on top faster than cooking in the middle, cover with foil. Punch holes in the foil to allow steam to escape. Pudding will be slightly set when ready.

When ready to serve, slice into servings and top with the whiskey sauce and candied pecans.

Make the sauce: In a large saucepan add the sugar and water. Heat over medium heat until the sugar is melted and medium brown in color. Working quickly, whisk in the butter, then the cream. Add the whiskey.

Stand away from the saucepan and light the whiskey so that it flames and burns off. If guests are present, it's a great conversation piece. If you don't want to flame the dessert, let the sauce bubble a minute or so. Add the salt and let it boil one minute more. Remove from heat.

Serves 16.

WHITE OR DARK CHOCOLATE CROISSANT BREAD PUDDING

Chef Tom McEachern contributes another great recipe. You don't have to be a chocolate lover to love this!

3 eggs
13/4 cups plus 2 tablespoons sugar
1 tablespoon plus 1/3 teaspoon vanilla extract
1 quart heavy cream

8 ounces white or dark chocolate, melted
12 to 13 large or 27 to 28 small croissants, cubed

In a large mixing bowl and using a whisk attachment, whip the eggs, 13/4 cups of the sugar, and the vanilla until thick and pale.

Heat the cream in a saucepan and whisk together with the chocolate. Slowly add the chocolate/cream to the egg mixture, combining completely. Stir the bread into the chocolate mixture and let it rest for 20 minutes, stirring occasionally so that bread is evenly soaked.

Preheat the oven to 350 degrees.

Spray one 13 x 9-inch baking dish with pan release spray and coat with the remaining 2 tablespoons sugar. Pour the pudding mixture into the prepared dish and bake for 25 to 35 minutes.

Serves 16 to 24.

PUMPKIN PIE ICE CREAM

This ice cream is delicious! Debbie Willyard, our chef for the photo shoot, offered this recipe for Second Helpings. *Gather your children and grandchildren in the kitchen when you make this one.*

1/2   gallon vanilla ice cream
1   (15-ounce) can Libby's pumpkin
  pie mix (not pure pumpkin)

1   box gingersnaps
1   jar caramel sauce

Allow the ice cream to soften enough for you to spoon it into a 13 x 9-inch glass baking dish. It should be soft, but not completely melted.

Spoon the pumpkin pie mix on top of the ice cream and swirl it in, being careful not to mix it.*

Crumble the desired number of gingersnaps and stir them into the pumpkin ice cream.

Stir about half the jar of caramel sauce into the ice cream mixture to create a ribbon effect.

Cover with plastic wrap and place in the freezer for at least 3 hours. Remove from the freezer 5 to 10 minutes before you are ready to serve. Scoop the ice cream into bowls and garnish with whole gingersnaps and more caramel sauce if you like.

Makes 3/4 gallon.

* The ice cream should have ribbons of orange throughout.

CHOCOLATE SORBET

A delicious frozen dessert from Tom McEachern. Sorbet is delicious whether it's summer or winter, and a chocolate sorbet is even better!

5	ounces bittersweet chocolate, chopped into small pieces	2 1/4	cups sugar
1 2/3	cups cocoa powder	2	cups milk
		1	quart water

Place the chocolate pieces in a large bowl.

In a medium bowl sift together the cocoa and sugar.

In a medium saucepan combine the cocoa and sugar mixture, the milk, and the water. Bring to a boil.

Once the liquid comes to a boil, pour it over the chopped chocolate. Gently fold in the mixture until the chocolate pieces melt completely. Place in an ice bath to cool and then refrigerate for at least 3 hours until you are ready to place it in an ice cream maker.

Churn according to the manufacturer's directions.

Makes 1 1/2 quarts.

LEMON CREAM DESSERT

Louise Kugler again gives us a great dessert recipe. She always bakes a dessert for employees at the store on their birthdays. Here is one of the favorites.

Filling:

1¹/2 cups sugar
¹/3 cup plus 1 tablespoon cornstarch
1¹/2 cups cold water
3 egg yolks, lightly beaten
3 tablespoons butter, cubed
2 teaspoons grated lemon peel
¹/2 cup lemon juice

Crust:

1¹/2 cups all-purpose flour
1¹/2 cups chopped walnuts
3/4 cup cold butter (1¹/2 sticks)

Cream cheese base:

1 (8-ounce) package cream cheese, softened
1 cup confectioners' sugar

Topping:

2 cups whole milk
2 (3.4-ounce) packages instant vanilla pudding mix
1 teaspoon vanilla extract
1 (16-ounce) carton frozen whipped topping, thawed

Make the filling: In a small saucepan combine the sugar and cornstarch. Gradually stir in the water until smooth. Bring to a boil. Cook and stir for 1 minute or until thickened. Remove from the heat and stir a small amount of the hot filling into the egg yolks. Add all of yolk mixture back into the hot filling, stirring constantly. Bring to a gentle boil, cooking and stirring for 1 minute. Remove from the heat and stir in the butter and lemon peel. Gently stir in the lemon juice and refrigerate until cool.

Preheat the oven to 350 degrees.

Make the crust: In a small bowl combine the flour and nuts. Cut the butter into the mixture until it resembles coarse crumbs. Press onto the bottom of a greased 13 x 9 x 2-inch baking dish. Bake for 15 to 20 minutes or until the edges are golden brown.

Remove from the oven and place on a wire rack to cool.

Make the base: In a small mixing bowl beat the cream cheese and confectioners' sugar until smooth. Carefully spread over the crust. Spread the cooled lemon mixture over the cream cheese mixture.

Make the topping: In a mixing bowl, using an electric mixer on low speed, beat the milk and pudding mixes for 2 minutes. Beat in the vanilla. Fold in half of the thawed whipped topping. Spread over the lemon layer. Spread with the remaining thawed whipped topping. Chill for at least 4 hours before cutting.

Serves 18 to 24.

CHOCOLATE TRUFFLES

Patti and Van Pearlberg sometimes entertain their guests at Christmas by making truffles. What a fun way to spend an evening and then return home with a box of little chocolate treasures!

1/2	cup whipping cream	3	tablespoons of your favorite liqueur
1/4	cup unsalted butter (1/2 stick)		Chopped nuts (pecans, walnuts, almonds, pistachio, hazelnuts), shredded coconut, and/or unsweetened cocoa powder for coating
1	tablespoon corn syrup		
10	ounces plus 1 pound bittersweet or semisweet (*not* unsweetened) chocolate, chopped		

Make the ganache* (filling): In a heavy, medium saucepan, stir the cream, butter, and corn syrup over medium heat until the butter melts and the mixture just begins to boil. Remove from the heat and add the 10 ounces of chopped chocolate, stirring until the entire mixture is melted and smooth.

Stir in the liqueur and then spread the mixture evenly in an 8-inch square pan. Freeze until firm. To make different-flavored truffles, divide the mixture among pans and then add a different liqueur to each pan.

Line a large baking sheet with waxed paper. Cut the chocolate into 1-inch squares, scooping out squares and forming them into balls. The heat from your hands will soften the chocolate so you can easily form the squares into round balls. Roll the chocolate balls in cocoa powder at this point if you want to give them a smoother outer appearance, but it's not necessary. Place the balls back into the freezer.

In a heavy saucepan melt the remaining 1 pound of chopped chocolate for the coating. Once melted, remove from the heat.

Remove the balls from the freezer. Working quickly, either submerge the balls into the chocolate or dip your hands and coat them by rolling in your hands.**

Place the coated balls back on the baking sheet and return to the freezer. Repeat this process twice, and then on the third time, while the chocolate coating is still wet, roll the truffle in the coating of your choice.

Makes 24 1-inch truffles.

VARIATION: We only do the dipping (coating) twice at our parties, but you get a better coating if you do it 3 times.

TIP: Place the finished product in small holiday papers and into holiday tins for gift giving.

* See the glossary.
** After you submerge your truffle in the chocolate, you might try retrieving it with a pointed thin wooden skewer. Any hole would be covered by the coating.

SUSAN'S TIRAMISU

An invitation to dinner at Susan and Tom Johnson's is reason for excitement. Susan has two hobbies now that they live in an empty nest. Cooking is one of them. Here's Susan's version of one of my favorite desserts.

6 to 7 large eggs, separated (pasteurized if possible, or use very fresh eggs without flaws or cracks)

1 1/2 cups sugar plus 1 1/2 teaspoons, divided

1 1/4 cups mascarpone cheese, at room temperature (you may substitute cream cheese for a portion of this, but not all)

3 tablespoons rum, divided

1 1/2 cups heavy cream, whipped

1/2 cup espresso, brewed or from an instant powder

3 to 4 packages Ladyfinger cookies, unfilled (usually found on bakery aisle or in freezer section)

1/2 ounce semisweet chocolate, grated

Separate the eggs into two mixing bowls. Beat the whites until stiff but not dry, and set aside.

Beat the egg yolks, gradually adding 1 1/2 cups of the sugar until you reach ribbon stage, and add the mascarpone cheese. Mix again until well blended and add 2 tablespoons of the rum. Fold in the beaten egg whites and then the whipped cream.

In a small bowl mix the espresso with the remaining 1 tablespoon rum and the remaining 1 1/2 teaspoons sugar.

Separate the ladyfingers and place a layer in the bottom of a 13 x 9-inch serving dish. Brush the ladyfingers with the espresso mixture and spread half of the mascarpone mixture over them. Repeat with another layer of ladyfingers, again brushing them with espresso. Follow with the remaining mascarpone mixture. Sprinkle the top with grated chocolate and chill for a minimum of 4 hours or overnight.

Serves 12.

FANTASY FUDGE

My friends Susan and Steve Tibbitts gave me this recipe. It is an old standard that deserves to be kept for posterity. Susan and Steve made this for friends at Christmas until they were up to 75 batches! Susan decided that was just too much for a full-time teacher to tackle. I sure hope she shared the recipe with the former recipients so they could make their own. If not, here it is.

3	sticks butter or margarine	1	(13-ounce) jar marshmallow creme
2	(5-ounce) cans evaporated milk		
6	cups sugar	4	teaspoons vanilla extract
2	(12-ounce) bags semisweet chocolate chips	1	cup chopped pecans

In a large saucepan combine the butter or margarine, evaporated milk, and sugar. Cook over medium heat, stirring constantly. Bring to a rolling boil. Reduce the heat and continue to boil for 5 full minutes.

Remove from the heat and stir in the chocolate chips and marshmallow creme. Add the vanilla and mix thoroughly. Stir in the nuts. Pour into a greased 13 x 9-inch pan. Refrigerate for at least 2 hours.

Cut into pieces with a pizza cutter. Keep refrigerated.

Makes 28 to 32 pieces of fudge.

LEDIES BARGO'S
PEANUT BUTTER FUDGE

Sally Litchfield, a columnist for the **Marietta Daily Journal,** *featured her dad's recipe one day. I saved it because I knew I would want to share it with you. Rev. and Mrs. Bargo raised three daughters and pastored churches in the area for more than twenty-nine years. Their recipes for family, life, and food are tried-and-true! Rev. Bargo sometimes stops by Gabriel's Desserts after he has hiked Kennesaw Mountain, which he does every day.*

3	cups sugar	1	(12-ounce) jar smooth peanut butter
2/3	cup milk		
2	tablespoons butter	1	teaspoon vanilla extract

Spray a dinner plate with a nonstick spray.

In a large saucepan bring the sugar, milk, and butter to a rolling boil. Boil for $4^{1}/_{2}$ minutes, turn off the heat, and stir in the peanut butter and vanilla extract. Remove from the heat and beat with a big spoon until the mixture loses its gloss and turns creamy. Immediately pour onto the prepared plate. Once the fudge begins to set (usually within 5 minutes), cut into small squares.

Makes 12 to 18 pieces.

LEDIES' TIP: It is better to make fudge on a clear, dry day. Don't overcook or it will be dry. Don't undercook or it will not set.

COMFORT ZONE

Getting out of my comfort zone wasn't my idea. I didn't like the results of some decisions I had made and I wanted my situation to change. One definition of insanity is "doing the same thing over and over and expecting a different result." I knew I had to do something different.

During the nineties' recession I started baking cakes out of my house with recipes from a lady who was already successful with them. When the demand for the cakes became greater than we could produce from our home and we could no longer survive working day jobs and baking at night, I had a decision to make. Keep the day job and quit baking or quit the day job, borrow some money, lease some space, and "bake them and they will come."

Selling a few desserts on Monday, Tuesday, and Wednesday and a lot on Thursday, Friday, and Saturday didn't pay the rent. Enter sandwiches, soups, vegetables, and cornbread.

When you can't seat but twenty people for lunch and you need to seat

sixty, it's time to move. We moved from 2150 square feet to 4800 square feet. It took angels in Gabriel's life in the form of Candler Properties and Northwest Bank and Trust, who believed in us, to accomplish our move. Along with a faithful crew of employees! For seven days we packed, moved, and unpacked, and what a beautiful store we moved into!

I asked Ed on the night before we opened the new store, what if no one comes? The next day people were lined up out the door. I could have wept with joy and relief.

We could cook the volume of food needed, but the serving system we had used in the old store didn't work with the new numbers of people—we were serving 350 to 400 people a day! Something had to change.

Nancy Tanase came to work for us on a part-time basis. Nancy was a nun who needed to leave her convent to care for her ill, widowed father. Nancy, our sweet, spirit-filled, intuitive Nancy, perceived that under the pressure of a new store, I was going to have a nervous breakdown. (Not far from the truth, except that I owed too much money to have a nervous breakdown and couldn't afford the time off.) Nancy began to bring me a Bible verse, every day, on a little sticky note and has continued to do so for three years now. I read those verses and they never fail to shore up my mind and emotions.

We did change some aspects of our serving system, and it seems to be working, for now.

During the three years the new Gabriel's has been open, many new opportunities have come my way. Writing two cookbooks, speaking at civic and church functions, cooking demonstrations at the Strand Theater for 400 to 500 people, TV appearances—things I never pictured myself doing—my philosophy has become: if the door opens, I'm going to do my homework and then walk through it.

The efforts of faithful employees, family, and friends have seen me through many challenges and continue to do so. Sometimes, courage is found only because others believe for you when you can't.

I met people I would never have met without the economic downturn in the nineties. I know people born into situations that required great courage to survive, and they have become heroes to me. It is downright exhilarating and confirms the perfection of God's creation when I see overcomers— people never giving up and beating the odds!

I can't tell you that I have found all of the answers to life's questions and dilemmas

My sweet Laura scooping the vegetables.

by escaping my comfort zone, but I can tell you I am not as afraid of a challenge as I used to be. I still have to take a deep breath—and pray—before I walk through a new door.

Life will grow you, if you let it.

Clockwise from top: Iced Green Tomato Pickles (page 243), Yellow Squash Pickles (page 240), and Sweet Pepper Relish (page 247)

THIS AND THAT

ASIAGO AND SAGE BISCUITS

We use this recipe at Gabriel's on our catering menu. These biscuits are especially good when served with chicken or pork. If you can't find Asiago, just substitute cheddar.

2	cups all-purpose flour, plus more for rolling out	1/4	cup or 4 tablespoons vegetable shortening
1	tablespoon baking powder	1 1/2	cups grated Asiago cheese (4 1/2 ounces) or use cheddar
1	teaspoon salt	1/4	cup thinly sliced fresh sage leaves (preferred) or 3 tablespoons dried
1/4	teaspoon paprika		
1	teaspoon sugar	2/3 to 1	cup whole milk
1/4	cup or 4 tablespoons butter, cut into small pieces	1	large egg, lightly beaten
		1	tablespoon heavy cream

Preheat the oven to 450 degrees.

In a medium bowl sift together the flour, baking powder, salt, paprika, and sugar. Using a pastry blender or two knives, cut in the butter and shortening until the mixture resembles coarse crumbs. Stir in the cheese and sage.

Add 2/3 cup of milk and stir with a fork until the mixture just comes together. If the dough does not seem pliable, add the remaining milk. Use enough milk to make a soft, puffy dough that's easy to roll out. Knead (fold dough over and press lightly with the heel of your hand about 5 to 6 times) on a lightly floured board. Too much handling will make the biscuits tough.

Roll or pat the dough to about 1/2-inch thick. Using a 1 1/4- to 1 1/2-inch biscuit cutter, cut out biscuits as close together as possible, dipping the cutter into flour each time to prevent sticking. Press straight down; don't twist.

Transfer the biscuits to a baking sheet. Place them close together if you want a biscuit with soft sides, and about 1 inch apart if you want crusty sides.

In a small bowl stir together the egg and cream. Lightly brush the top of each biscuit with the egg wash. Bake about 8 to 10 minutes and rotate the pan. Bake an additional 8 to 10 minutes until golden brown. Move to a wire rack to cool. Serve warm or at room temperature.

Makes 20 (2-inch) biscuits.

BÉCHAMEL SAUCE

A simple white sauce made with flour, butter, and milk that is the base for many creamy dishes, including gratins, macaroni and cheese, creamed spinach, and the cheese sauce for the cauliflower au gratin on page 124.

6¹/2	tablespoons butter		¹/4	heaping teaspoon white pepper
¹/2	onion, chopped			Pinch of nutmeg
³/4	cup plus 1 tablespoon flour		2¹/2	ounces Swiss cheese
3	cups plus 3 tablespoons milk		¹/3	cup Parmesan cheese
1¹/4	teaspoon salt			

In a saucepan melt the butter over medium heat. Add the onion and sauté until tender. Turn the heat down and whisk in the flour to make a white roux. Cook 1 ¹/2 to 2 minutes. Do not brown the flour. Slowly whisk in the milk, continuing to stir until thickened. Add the salt, pepper, and nutmeg. Add the cheeses, stirring until smooth. Strain out the onion and use the sauce immediately or store in the refrigerator.

Makes 1 quart.

CANDIED GRAPEFRUIT PEEL

This is one of those recipes that we don't want to lose. Alexis Amaden's great-grandmother Kersting made this old-school sour patch candy. You can use your favorite citrus peel: orange, lemon, lime, or grapefruit.

1 pound grapefruit rind (4 halves)	2 1/2 cups sugar, divided

Cut the grapefruit rind into thin strips using scissors. Put the strips in a medium saucepan and cover with water. Bring to a boil and cook about 20 minutes. Pour the water off and repeat the same process 4 more times, each time cooking and pouring the water off.

The fifth time pour out the water and stir in 2 cups of the sugar. Cook over low heat, stirring gently until the sugar melts. Place the candied grapefruit pieces into a bag filled with the remaining 1/2 cup sugar. Shake the pieces to coat them with the sugar. Once coated, cool them on a cookie sheet. Store in an airtight container.

Makes 1 to 2 cups.

NOTE: These candy pieces make an excellent garnish for your favorite desserts.

CHEESE BISCUITS

My Bible study friend Gail Schwartz brought these biscuits one night when we had soup and salad to kick off the study of Revelation. They were delicious with her beef and barley soup (page 45).

Nonstick cooking spray
1 cup self-rising flour*
3 tablespoons mayonnaise

1/2 cup buttermilk
1 cup grated sharp cheddar cheese
Garlic salt to taste

Preheat the oven to 425 degrees.

Spray muffins tins with nonstick spray.

In a mixing bowl add the self-rising flour, mayonnaise, buttermilk, and cheddar cheese and mix with a spoon. Spoon into the muffin tins and sprinkle the tops with garlic salt. Bake 12 to 15 minutes.

Makes 6 biscuits.

NOTE: If you're serving a large crowd, just double this recipe.

* If you don't have self-rising flour, add 2 teaspoons baking powder and 1/2 teaspoon salt per cup of all-purpose flour.

EVELYN ELLIOTT'S SOUTHERN BISCUITS

Evelyn, or Ebbie, as the grandchildren call her, serves these with her famous fried chicken (page 88). They will melt in your mouth.

Wooden bowl*
3 1/2 cups self-rising flour

1/2 cup Crisco or any solid vegetable shortening
1 cup buttermilk

Preheat the oven to 450 degrees.

Sift the flour into the bowl. Create a well in the middle of the flour.

Cut the shortening into small cubes and add to the flour. Using your fingers, pinch the Crisco into the flour until the mixture looks like coarse meal, pulling the flour in from the sides of the bowl to be incorporated. Make a well again and add the buttermilk. Stir with a fork until the mixture forms a ball. Add more buttermilk if the dough doesn't come together. The dough is the right consistency when it doesn't stick to your fingers anymore.

Turn the dough onto a floured surface and knead.** Roll or pat out the dough 1/4-inch-thick for thin, crusty biscuits and 1/2-inch-thick for softer biscuits.

Using a biscuit cutter, press straight down into the dough without twisting. Place the biscuits on an ungreased cookie sheet, close together for biscuits with soft sides and about an inch apart for biscuits with crusty sides. Bake for 10 to 12 minutes.

Makes 12 (3-inch) biscuits.

NOTE: If you want to mix these and freeze some for later, double this batch and bake half of the biscuits for only 8 minutes (not browning). Cool on the pan. Freeze on a cookie sheet and then store in self-sealing bags in the freezer. Remove the biscuits from the freezer and allow them to defrost before reheating and browning lightly in the oven.

* I still have my grandmother's wooden bowl, and I use it when I am making a large batch of biscuits, but if you don't have a wooden bowl, a glass or enamel one will work just fine.

** Fold the dough over and press lightly with the heel of your hand 5 to 6 times. Too much handling makes the biscuits tough.

YELLOW SQUASH PICKLES

From Evelyn Elliott's pantry.

8   cups thinly sliced yellow squash
2   cups thinly sliced yellow onions
2   green bell peppers, sliced
1   red bell pepper, sliced*
    Handful of salt
2¹/2   cups sugar

2   cups apple cider vinegar
2   teaspoons mustard seeds
2   teaspoons celery seeds
¹/2   teaspoon dry mustard
    Pinch of turmeric, for color

In a large enamel or stainless steel pan that can be heated on the stove, layer the squash, onions, and peppers. Sprinkle a handful of salt over the vegetables. Cover the vegetables with ice cubes and let stand for one hour.

While the vegetables are standing prepare the seasoning blend. In a medium bowl mix the sugar, vinegar, mustard and celery seeds, and the turmeric, and stir to blend.

Drain the ice water off of the vegetables and pour the sugar mixture over them. Place the pan on the stove and bring the mixture to a boil. Reduce the heat to simmer and cook for 10 minutes, until sugar dissolves. If you have to stir the vegetables, be careful not to break up the slices.

While the vegetables are simmering prepare the jars and rings. See page 247 for jar preparation. While the jars are still hot, fill them with the hot vegetables and liquid, leaving 1/2 inch head space in the jar. Immediately place the seal and ring on each jar and hand-tighten the lid. Cool for several hours on the counter, listening for the "ping" that let's you know the jar is properly sealed.

Any jars with rounded seals have not sealed properly. Refrigerate any jars that do not seal properly and use within 10 to 14 days

Makes 6 pints.

NOTE: Store opened jars of squash pickles in the refrigerator.

* Substitute with an additional green bell pepper, if you prefer.

GRANOLA

Mo Bednarowski, our catering manager, is adept at both savory and dessert dishes at Gabriel's, but the contribution of this granola recipe wins her rave reviews from our customers. We bag it for sale and use it on our yogurt and fruit dish for breakfast. This recipe doubles or triples for a large family or gift giving.

	Nonstick cooking spray	1/2	cup pecans
4	cups oats	1/2	cup walnuts
2	cups coconut	3/4	cups canola oil
2	cups sliced almonds	3/4	cups honey
3/4	cups whole almonds	1	cups Craisins

Preheat the oven to 325 degrees.

Heavily spray sheet pans with a nonstick spray, covering completely, and set aside.

In a large bowl combine the oats, coconut, sliced and whole almonds, pecans, and walnuts.

In a medium bowl whisk together the oil and honey.

Pour the wet mixture over the dry ingredients and thoroughly mix to ensure that all dry ingredients are covered and the wet mix is evenly distributed.

Evenly spread the mixture out on the sheet pans, being careful not to press the ingredients into the pan.

Bake for about 30 minutes, tossing every 12 minutes, until the granola is golden brown.

Remove the granola from the oven and add the Craisins, evenly distributing them among your sheet pans. Toss the granola to incorporate the Craisins. Smooth out again and allow to cool to room temperature on the sheet pans.

Store in an airtight container for up to 4 weeks.

Makes 10 to 12 cups.

NANCY'S
ICED GREEN TOMATO PICKLES

My friend—sister in my heart—Nancy Dorsey, a member of my "Birthday Club," gave me this recipe. During the summer, along with being a very successful real estate agent, mother, grandmother, and Sunday school teacher, Nancy freezes fresh vegetables and makes these green tomato pickles. When it is her time to have us for dinner, she knows we're going to request her fried okra, sliced cantaloupe, cornbread, frozen-fresh-from-the-garden vegetables, and these green tomato pickles. I heard it through the grapevine that my cousin, Paula Deen, puts these on her grilled cheese sandwich. So, roll up your sleeves and go for it . . . they're worth it!

3 cups pickling lime*	1¹/2 teaspoons ground ginger
2 gallons water	1¹/2 teaspoons allspice
7 to 8 pounds of medium-size, firm green tomatoes (no red showing), washed	1¹/2 teaspoons celery seed
	1¹/2 teaspoons mace
7¹/2 pounds sugar	1¹/2 teaspoons cinnamon or 1¹/2 sticks of cinnamon
4¹/2 pints (72 ounces) apple cider vinegar	Clean glass canning jars with new lids and rings**
1¹/2 teaspoons whole cloves	

In a large plastic tub, dissolve the pickling lime in the water. Slice each tomato into 4 to 5 slices, not too thin, so that the slices stay intact. Put the tomatoes into the liquid, making sure that all slices are covered with water, and let soak for 24 hours.

After 24 hours drain the lime water from the tomatoes. Add fresh water to the container, covering the tomatoes. Soak 4 hours, changing the water every hour. Drain the fresh water off the tomatoes.

During the last 30 minutes to 1 hour of the fresh water soaking time, mix the sugar, vinegar, cloves, ginger, allspice, celery seed, mace, and cinnamon in a large kettle. Over medium heat, bring the mixture to a boil, and stir to be sure all the sugar has melted and the spices are mixed. Gently add the sliced tomatoes to the hot liquid. Let stand overnight.

Next day, bring to a gentle boil and cook, boiling for 1 hour. During this boiling time prepare your canning jars, lids, and rings according to the manufacturer's directions, washing them in hot soapy water and rinsing well. Check the jars for chips and the lids and rings for any dents or rust, as these will prevent them from sealing correctly. Do not use other glass food jars, such as mayonnaise or pickle jars, since the seals are more likely to fail and the jars may break.

With a large slotted spoon, place the slices in the jars, filling to the top. Pour the hot syrup over the slices, covering them completely. Immediately place the ring on top of the jar as you finish filling each one. With a clean, hot cloth, wipe off any liquid you might have spilled on the jar. Place the ring firmly on the jar and leave on the countertop to cool. You may hear little pings as the lids seal.

As they are cooling, step back and admire your work often, as you have finished a two-day process! But be careful. Giving these as gifts can become habit-forming for the recipients. Your friends will ask if you're making tomato pickles this year.

When cooled, label and date the jars and store in a cool, dry, dark place.

Makes 8 to 10 pints.

TIP: Refrigerate jars of pickles after opening.

TIP: Canned foods properly sealed will keep for several years. If sealed properly, the lid will have to be removed by using a bottle opener. If not sealed properly, there will be signs of spoilage. Do not eat the food if there is an odor, foam on top, or mold. Discard any other jars that might spurt when opened, have bulging lids, or any that have leaked.

---

* pickling lime—sometimes I can find it in grocery stores during the summer. I also searched the Internet and found it at www.canningpantry.com.

** According to Nancy, her plans for the pickles determine the size jars. For gifts she uses half-pint jars (I am sometimes the recipient of one of these and have lobbied for larger jars). For her own personal use she uses quart jars. Jars can be used from year to year if they are not chipped, but it is safer to use new rings and lids each time. Jars, lids, and rings can be purchased at the grocery store.

REMOULADE SAUCE

Donya Morris shares this recipe with many folks, and I was lucky enough to be one of them. It is delicious with Glynda's Roasted Salmon (page 94).

1/2	cup mayonnaise		1/2	cup chopped parsley
1/2	cup spicy mustard		1/2	teaspoon lemon juice
1	tablespoon Worcestershire sauce		1	tablespoon paprika
1	teaspoon Tabasco sauce		1/2	teaspoon salt
1/2	cup chopped green onions		1/2	teaspoon pepper
2	tablespoons chopped or pressed garlic			

In a medium bowl mix the mayonnaise, mustard, Worcestershire, Tabasco, green onions, garlic, parsley, lemon juice, paprika, salt, and pepper until combined. Chill until ready to serve.

Makes 1 1/2 to 2 cups.

SWEET PEPPER RELISH

Mrs. Flo Black, eighty-nine years old, has been making sweet pepper relish for years now. She lives in a retirement residence, so everything is considerably downsized for her, but she still finds the time and space to make this sweet pepper relish for the three generations who cherish her recipe and appreciate her handiwork. You keep it up, Mrs. Black!

4	cups ground unpeeled cucumbers (about 4 medium cucumbers)	1/4	cup salt
1	cup ground green bell pepper (about 2 medium peppers)	3 1/2	cups sugar
1/2	cup ground red bell pepper (about 1 medium pepper)	2	cups white vinegar
3	cups finely diced celery	1	tablespoon celery seeds
		1	tablespoon mustard seeds
		6	pint jars, rings, and lids

In a large bowl combine the cucumbers, bell peppers, and celery. Sprinkle with the salt and cover with cold water. Let the mixture stand for 4 hours.

Drain thoroughly in a colander. Using your hands, press out all remaining liquid.

In a 4-quart saucepan combine the sugar, vinegar, and celery and mustard seeds, and bring to a boil, stirring until the sugar is dissolved. Stir in the drained vegetables. Simmer 10 minutes.

While the vegetables are simmering prepare the jars, rings, and lids according to the manufacturer's directions, washing them in hot soapy water and rinsing well. Check the jars for chips and the lids and rings for any dents or rust, as these will prevent them from creating an airtight seal.

After cooking the vegetables for 10 minutes, immediately pack them and the remaining liquid in clean, hot jars, leaving 1/2-inch head space. To ensure proper sealing process the jars in a boiling water bath for 10 minutes.

Turn off the heat and allow the water to cool enough to safely handle the jars. With tongs remove the jars from the water and allow to cool. As the jars begin to cool, you may hear a ping from the lids as they seal or see a slight indention in the lids. Dry off the jars (you may remove the rings if you like). Label and date the jars and store in a cool, dry, dark place until ready to enjoy.

Makes about 6 pints.

NOTE: The container used for the water bath must be tall enough for the water level to be several inches over the tops of the jars during the entire process, with room for the water to boil freely. A tight-fitting lid for the container is necessary, along with a metal rack with dividers to separate the jars and keep them off the bottom of the canners. The rack keeps the jars upright and separated during the processing and allows the boiling water to totally surround each jar. The filled jars should be placed in the water bath when the water is hot but not boiling. Once the water is brought to the boiling point, it should be kept boiling during the entire process. With the lid on, boil the filled jars for approximately 10 minutes.

NOTE: Using other glass food jars, such as mayonnaise jars, is not recommended, as the seals are more apt to fail or the jars to break. Canned foods properly sealed will keep for several years. If properly sealed, it will be apparent when you open it for use. The lid will have to be removed by lifting with a bottle opener or pried off in some other way. If the jar was not sealed properly, there will be signs of spoilage of the food: an odor or foam on top or mold. Do not eat the food, and discard any other jars that might spurt when opened, have bulging lids, or any that have leaked.

TIP: Electric and manual food grinders can be purchased on the Internet. Mrs. Black uses the food grinder attachment that fits her KitchenAid mixer. Check with the manufacturer of your tabletop mixer to see if they offer a separate attachment for your brand.

NOTE: If you buy a home canner or borrow one, follow the manufacturer's directions. You may use a steam pressure canner if you have one or one is available to you, but steam canning is not necessary with high-acid foods such as cucumbers and peppers.

SALSA CRUDA

This is another good recipe from Tom McEachern. He serves this salsa cruda over fish at Ray's on the River. Gabriel's is serving it over our salmon cakes.

2	pints red grape and/or yellow teardrop tomatoes, halved	4	basil leaves, chiffonade*
2	teaspoons lemon juice	1/2	teaspoon cracked pepper
1	clove garlic, minced	1/2	teaspoon kosher salt
1/4	cup minced red onion	3	tablespoons extra-virgin olive oil

In a medium bowl mix the halved tomatoes, lemon juice, garlic, red onion, basil, pepper, and salt. Refrigerate for at least one hour.

Spoon the mixture on top of fish and drizzle the olive oil over the fish.

Makes 18 to 24 servings.

NOTE: At Gabriel's we mix all the ingredients before serving and ladle the salsa cruda over the salmon cakes.

* See the glossary on page 267 for tips to creating the perfect chiffonade.

SWEET POTATO BISCUITS

Our executive chef, Brian Charles, contributed this recipe. When Gabriel's caters our pork tenderloin, we always suggest serving it with this biscuit and the barbecue sauce that accompanies the pork. We cut the biscuits just about the size of a slice of tenderloin. You can find George Brown's Pork Tenderloin with Barbecue Sauce on page 114 in Cooking in the South with Johnnie Gabriel.

2	cups cooked, mashed sweet potatoes		Pinch of baking soda
1	stick unsalted butter, melted	3	tablespoons sugar
1 1/4	cups milk	1 1/4	teaspoons cinnamon
5	cups self-rising flour*	2	eggs, beaten
		1	ounce water

Preheat the oven to 400 degrees.

In a large bowl mix together the sweet potatoes, butter, and the milk until well blended. Stir in the flour, baking soda, sugar, and cinnamon. Shape the dough into a ball and knead about 10 times on a floured surface.

Roll the dough 1-inch thick and cut with a 2- or 3-inch floured biscuit cutter. Press straight down with the cutter. Don't twist as you're cutting.

In a small bowl mix the eggs with the water and brush over the tops of the biscuits. Bake on a greased or parchment-lined pan for 15 to 20 minutes.

Makes 20 2 1/2-inch biscuits.

* Make your own self-rising flour from all-purpose flour. Mix 1 cup all-purpose flour with 3 teaspoons baking powder and 1/2 teaspoon salt.

Herb Tenderloin Sauce

Serve this sauce with the beef tenderloin on page 80.

- 2 green onions, chopped
- 2 tablespoons chopped parsley
- 1 tablespoon flour
- 1 tablespoon brandy
- 1 tablespoon lemon juice
- 1 tablespoon tomato paste
- 2 teaspoons Dijon mustard
- 1 teaspoon seasoned pepper
- 1 teaspoon Fines Herbes or Herbes de Provence*
- 1 teaspoon paprika
- 1 teaspoon Worcestershire sauce (white wine preferably)
- 1 teaspoon capers
- 1 teaspoon green peppercorns
- 1 teaspoon anchovy paste
- 1/2 teaspoon salt
- 1/2 teaspoon curry powder
- 1 cup whipping cream
- 4 ounces cold butter
- 2 to 3 tablespoons sour cream

In a medium bowl combine the onions, parsley, flour, brandy, lemon juice, tomato paste, mustard, pepper, Fines Herbes, paprika, Worcestershire sauce, capers, peppercorns, anchovy paste, salt, and curry powder. Using a hand mixer (Magic Wand), blend until the mixture resembles the consistency of a thick mayonnaise. Place in an airtight container and leave at room temperature for 12 hours. This can be refrigerated for up to 2 or 3 weeks.

When ready to serve, bring 1 cup whipping cream to boil for 1 to 2 minutes. Add the herb mixture, whisking, and return to low boil for 1 to 2 minutes. The mixture will get heavy. Reduce the heat and add the cold butter, one ounce at a time, whisking into the sauce. Whisk in 2 to 3 tablespoons of sour cream. Reheat through without boiling.

Makes enough sauce for a tenderloin that serves 12.

* Fines Herbes and Herbes de Provence are in the spice aisle at most grocery stores.

SWEET AND SOUR MUSTARD SAUCE

Randy and Pam Webb serve this sauce with grilled pork tenderloin or with turkey. It's another one of their favorites.

Nonstick cooking spray
1/4 cup apple cider vinegar
1/4 cup ketchup
1/4 cup orange juice concentrate
1/4 cup honey
1/4 cup orange or apricot marmalade
1/4 cup firmly packed brown sugar

1 teaspoon Montreal steak seasoning or lemon pepper
1/2 teaspoon dry mustard
1/4 teaspoon salt
Pinch of cayenne pepper
3/4 cup yellow mustard

In a medium saucepan sprayed with nonstick spray, mix the vinegar, ketchup, orange juice concentrate, honey, marmalade, and brown sugar.

Add the steak seasoning, dry mustard, salt, and cayenne pepper, and bring to a boil for 1 to 2 minutes. Add the yellow mustard and heat thoroughly.

Makes 2 1/4 cups.

YEAST ROLLS

Another good recipe from Liz Cole. Is there anything she doesn't cook well?

1	cup vegetable shortening	3	packages Rapid Rise yeast
1	cup sugar	3	eggs, slightly beaten
1	tablespoon salt	6 to 8	cups sifted all-purpose flour
1	cup boiling water	1/2	cup margarine or butter, melted

In a large mixing bowl use an electric mixer to cream the shortening, sugar, and salt. Pour the boiling water into a samll bowl and set aside to cool.

When the water has cooled dissolve the yeast and mix well. Add the eggs and flour into the shortening mixture.

Add the flour until the mass becomes manageable. Knead gently in the bowl for 1 minute. The side of the bowl should be lightly floured to allow the dough to rise. Cover the bowl with a damp cloth and let the dough rise. Quick yeast will take about an hour.

Place the dough on a floured surface and knead again. Roll out and cut with a biscuit cutter.* Dip the rolls in the margarine and place on greased baking pans.

Allow the rolls to rise again in a warm spot for 30 minutes to an hour, until they have doubled in size.

Preheat the oven to 350 degrees.

Bake until golden brown, about 15 minutes.

Makes 5 to 6 dozen.

NOTE: If you're not ready to bake the rolls, the pan can be stored in the refrigerator. Remove one hour before baking time to allow the dough to rise.

TIP: To help the dough rise faster, put the bowl on top of the clothes dryer while it is running.

---

* Liz uses a small juice glass that has been floured. When you cut out the rolls, push straight down into the dough. Twisting the glass as you cut down will seal the edges of the roll, which will prevent them from rising.

BLACKENING SPICE

Seafood is huge at Ray's on the River, so you know Tom McEachern's recipe is great.

7	tablespoons plus 1½ teaspoons paprika	1	tablespoon garlic powder
1½	teaspoons dried basil	1	tablespoon salt
1½	teaspoons dried oregano	1½	teaspoons black pepper
1	tablespoon onion powder	1	tablespoon white pepper
		1	tablespoon cayenne pepper

In a medium bowl combine the paprika, basil, oregano, onion and garlic powders, salt, and peppers. Pour the mixture into a tightly sealed container.

Makes almost 1 cup.

Gabriel's Garlicky Croutons

Gabriel's makes these in-house to serve with our Caesar salad. Customers always comment on them. I think ours are interesting because we use all of the leftover breads, including the croissants, which make my favorite croutons.

2 pounds plus 6 ounces old bread	3/4 cup chopped garlic in oil
4 tablespoons Mrs. Dash seasoning	3 ounces blended oil (combination of olive and vegetable oil)
3/4 cup dried basil	
3 1/2 tablespoons seasoning salt	

Preheat the oven to 325 degrees.

Cut the bread into 1-inch squares. In a large bowl combine the Mrs. Dash seasoning, basil, and seasoning salt and stir to combine. In a medium bowl whisk together the garlic and the oil. Add the oil mixture to the seasoning mix and toss the bread to coat well.

Spread the seasoned bread out on 2 full-size sheet pans. Bake for 20 minutes, turning the pan and stirring the croutons a couple of times during the baking process to ensure even baking.

Makes 2 pounds 4 ounces.

HOLLANDAISE SAUCE

This is the sauce Marshall and Cindy Dye use to top off their Oysters Rockefeller with a Twist. Use it whenever serving hollandaise.

2	egg yolks	1/2	cup firm butter, divided	
3	tablespoons lemon juice			

In a small saucepan add the egg yolks and lemon juice and whisk until well combined.

Add $1/4$ cup of the butter and stir over low heat until the butter is melted.

Add the remaining $1/4$ cup butter, stirring until the sauce thickens. Keep the heat low to give the eggs time to cook and thicken the sauce without curdling.

Makes $3/4$ to 1 cup.

RICE PILAF

Randy Winns, an executive chef at Gabriel's served this simple and tasty dish.

2	cups rice	1	tablespoon butter
4	cups water	1	carrot, diced
2	tablespoons oil	2	stalks of celery, diced
1	tablespoon salt	1	whole onion, diced

In a 2-quart saucepan, bring the rice, water, oil, and salt to a boil. Cover and cook for 20 minutes.

In a medium skillet over medium heat, melt the butter and add the carrots, celery, and onion. Sauté until translucent. Add to the cooked rice. Serve immediately.

Serves 6 to 8.

Black Bean Avocado Salsa

Chef Eric Rebo contributed this recipe. I think you'll love it. It has two of my favorite ingredients: black beans and avocado. Serve this over fresh fish—salmon, sea bass, and trout are a few of my favorites.

1 3/4	cups cooked black beans	1/3	cup diced scallions
2	large avocadoes	1	tablespoon diced jalapeño
3/4	cup fresh diced tomatoes	3/4	teaspoon cumin
1/2	bunch cilantro, finely diced	3/4	teaspoon chili powder
1/4	cup minced shallots	1/2	cup honey
1	cup apple cider vinegar	1 1/2	cups olive oil
3/4	teaspoon crushed red pepper*	1/2	cup sour cream

Place half of the black beans, half of the avocadoes, and half of the tomatoes in a blender.

Add the cilantro, shallots, vinegar, crushed red pepper, scallions, jalapeño, cumin, chili powder, honey, olive oil, and sour cream, and puree.

Add the remaining beans, avocadoes, and tomatoes, and pulse once or twice, leaving a fair amount of texture to the salsa. Depending on the size of your blender, you may have to do this in batches.

Makes 6 cups.

ALTERNATE METHOD: Create a vinaigrette by emulsifying the ingredients in the blender. Allow the vinaigrette to sit for at least 24 hours to fuse the flavors.

---

* There's a lot of heat in this recipe. I suggest that you use half of the spices before you add the last half of the beans, avocadoes, and tomatoes, and taste the mixture. If you want more heat, add the remaining spices.

ROASTED SHALLOT VINAIGRETTE

Chef Eric Rebo of Gem City Bar and Grill says this vinaigrette is great over fresh spinach or a mesculin mix with toasted or candied almonds, pecans, or walnuts.

4   slices bacon, diced
1   cup sliced shallots
1/4   cup sliced garlic
2   tablespoons firmly packed brown sugar

2   cups apple cider vinegar
2   tablespoons Dijon mustard
    Salt and pepper to taste

In a medium sauté pan cook the diced bacon over medium heat. Remove the bacon to a paper towel to drain. Add the shallots to the bacon grease and caramelize over medium heat, cooking until they begin to turn brown and get soft. Add the garlic and stir, being careful not to burn.

Add the brown sugar, vinegar, mustard, and the salt and pepper, and simmer until the sugar has melted. Cool and place in a blender. Puree. Add the crumbled bacon and serve immediately or store in the refrigerator until ready to use.

Makes 3 cups.

CILANTRO MAYONNAISE

Chef Eric Rebo suggests putting this on a croissant with a blackened chicken breast* and garnishing with shredded lettuce.

1	cup finely diced cilantro	1 1/2	tablespoons balsamic vinegar
2 2/3	cups mayonnaise	1/2	heaping teaspoon onion powder
1	27.5 can roasted red peppers	1/2	teaspoon red pepper flakes
1/2	heaping teaspoon cumin	1/2	heaping teaspoon garlic
1/2	heaping teaspoon chili powder	3	tablespoons plus 1 teaspoon honey
1/3	cup sour cream		

In a large bowl add the cilantro, mayonnaise, red peppers, cumin, chili powder, sour cream, vinegar, onion powder, red pepper flakes, garlic, and honey, and whisk to combine. Place in a tightly sealed container and refrigerate.

Makes 3 1/2 to 4 cups.

* See the recipe for blackening spice on page 255.

CHILTON'S EGGNOG

Pat and Red Chilton have hosted a Christmas party at their home for the last thirty-plus years. The Chiltons offer their guests a joyful celebration with good friends, good food, and their holiday eggnog.

15	eggs, separated	3/4 to 1 cup dark rum (based on personal taste)	
1/2	teaspoon salt		
2 1/4	cups sugar, divided	1/4	cup dry sherry
3 3/4	cups to 1 quart bourbon (based on personal taste)	1	quart heavy cream
		1	quart whole milk
			Ground nutmeg

In a large mixing bowl use an electric mixer to beat the egg yolks until frothy. Add the salt and 1/4 cup of the sugar and continue beating the yolks until they are thick and creamy and the sugar has dissolved. While still beating the yolks gradually add the bourbon in a slow, steady stream. Continue to beat the mixture and slowly add the rum and then the sherry. Place the mixture in the refrigerator while you prepare the heavy cream.

In a large mixing bowl beat the cream until it holds a stiff peak. Do not overbeat it. Pour the yolk mixture over the heavy cream and fold to blend.

Pour the whole milk into the cream mixture and stir.

In another large bowl beat the egg whites until stiff. Slowly add the remaining 2 cups sugar, 1 tablespoon at a time, until incorporated. Pour the whites over the cream mixture and fold to blend. It's not necessary to completely blend all the whites, but don't leave large chunks unblended. Refrigerate overnight.

To serve, stir with a spoon to blend any part of the mixture that may have separated and pour into a chilled punch bowl. Sprinkle with ground nutmeg.

Makes 35 to 40 servings.

TIP: The addition of the alcohol cooks the eggs, and small pieces of cooked yolk may form. To remove the cooked yolks, pour the mixture through a strainer into another container.

ABOUT THE AUTHOR

Johnnie Gabriel started baking cakes alongside her grandmother as a young girl in south Georgia. Today, Johnnie is known as Atlanta's "Cake Lady" for her mouth-watering red velvet cupcakes, award-winning wedding cakes, and other delectable desserts.

In 1996, Johnnie and Ed Gabriel expanded their successful dessert business into Gabriel's Restaurant and Bakery, a popular restaurant serving homemade southern comfort food for breakfast, lunch, and dinner. On any given day, you're likely to see Johnnie greeting customers and serving up fresh veggies, cornbread, and sweet tea.

Johnnie lives in Marietta, Georgia surrounded by friends and family who continue to support her along life's journey.

Double-Fudge Chocolate Cupcakes with Peanut Butter Buttercream Frosting (page 116)

ACKNOWLEDGMENTS

I can't imagine completing a project such as *Second Helpings* without a host of family, friends, coworkers, and professionals (who become like family) working side by side with me, supporting me in thought and deed. I know there must be many small towns across the world that offer the feeling of true community life. One that works and hopes for well-being for all. I am so proud to be a part of this Marietta/Cobb/metro Atlanta community. Without this community, along with Gabriel's Desserts and its employees, I doubt that either *Cooking in the South* or *Second Helpings* would have come into existence.

As you glance through *Second Helpings,* you will see there are a host of good Marietta cooks who shared their recipes with me, and I thank them from the bottom of my heart. Their fare and generosity truly encourage "second helpings." Tom and Dawn McEachern not only shared their recipes, but surrendered their home for four days for the photo shoot. What an exhilarating adventure to see Chef Debbie Willyard brilliantly prepare these recipes so that food stylist Libbie Summers could work her artistic magic for photographer Ron Manville to shoot them and forever preserve the proof of their existence and beauty for you, our reader, to inspire you to COOK! All the while, my editor, guide, and encourager of many months, Heather Skelton, was steering us through the week, marveling at the number of my friends who came through the door right on time with dishes prepared for the shoot. The savory and pastry chefs at Gabriel's prepped, cooked, and baked dishes for me and still fed 350–400 Gabriel's customers a day.

Joel Miller, my publisher at Thomas Nelson, who effortlessly, threw out the phrase "second helpings" for the title (which I immediately loved!), graciously sent Heather Skelton down from Nashville for a week to hold my hand (and wash a lot of dishes) through the photo shoot. The clever and creative team, Jason Jones and Kristi Henson, integral members of my Nashville "family," seem to have endless ideas and energy when it comes to promoting my first book *Cooking in the South, Second Helpings,* and me! The designers who so artfully put

Second Helpings together, Kristen Vasgaard and Walter Petrie, you've made this Marietta cook smile.

The sales crew, Heather McCullough, Monica Jones, Susan Plunkett, and Mindy Henderson at Brand New Day Marketing, and many, many more who've worked their magic behind the scenes to enthusiastically promote me, I am so grateful!

During these many months of "birthing" a book, my husband, Ed, only *heard* about delicious dishes, since I had no time to cook them. I appreciate his patience. To my family and friends, who often heard "I can't talk right now. I'm working on the book," thank you for indulging and loving me, especially Stephanie and Laura, my daughters, who have always had my ear . . . and what a loving and adventurous journey motherhood has been! To my "sister in my heart" and coworker at Gabriel's, Pam Addicks, who held down the fort the many days I wasn't at Gabriel's, and to Liz Cole, my friend and organizational guru, thanks is not enough! Just a promise to try to follow you all's example of a faithful friend. Liz, Maria Geros, and Nancy van Brenk, thank you for your hours of editing and questions so that we could submit a worthy manuscript.

Once again, Paula Deen has taken time to pen the foreword for me. All of America loves you, Paula, for the generous heart that orchestrates your life and work. Thank you for your generous sharing, love, and faith in me.

Most of all, thank you, fellow cooks and readers of cookbooks . . . joy, peace, and bountiful blessings to all who go through the pages of this book.

Glossary

al dente: firm to the bite. The term is usually used of pasta, to indicate a short cooking time so the pasta is fully cooked but still slightly firm in texture. To cook pasta al dente, bring salted water to a boil on high heat (4 to 6 quarts per pound of dry pasta) and stir in the pasta. Allow the water to return to a boil; then reduce the heat to medium to medium-high, stirring a couple of times to prevent pasta from sticking together. Do not overstir, as this will make the pasta sticky and mushy. After a minute, remove a piece of the pasta, let it cool a few seconds, and take a bite. You should be able to bite through the pasta, but it should still be firm and slightly chewy. If the pasta is still hard, allow it to cook another minute, and then remove another piece to test. Continue testing every minute until the pasta is fully cooked but not soft. (If using boxed or packaged pasta, simply cook according to the package instructions.) Once the pasta is al dente, drain immediately. Do not allow the pasta to sit in the water. Tip: Some cooks add a tablespoon of oil to the pot, to keep the pasta from sticking together.

au gratin: topped with a brown crust. Au gratin dishes are usually baked and topped with a crust (usually made with cheese and breadcrumbs). The dish is often placed under the broiler until the crust is golden.

baking blind (also known as *blind-baking* or *prebaking*): baking a pie crust or pastry before it is filled

béarnaise sauce: a sauce made with butter and egg yolks, and typically seasoned with scallions, vinegar, wine, and herbs and spices (our recipe omits the vinegar)

béchamel: a rich white sauce, often used as a base for creamy dishes or other sauces

beef Wellington: beef fillets covered with pâtè and baked wrapped in puff pastry

biscotti: crisp Italian twice-baked cookies, often made with almonds, or sometimes pine nuts, and flavored with anise

blackening spice: a blend of spices used to add a smoky flavor to fish, seafood, meat, poultry, vegetables, and other recipes (see recipe on page 255). When cooking meats or fish, blackening spice is usually applied thickly just before pan searing the pieces in a hot skillet.

blanch: to cook or briefly plunge a food (usually a fruit or vegetable) into boiling water, and then plunge into iced water or place under cold running water. Blanching is performed to loosen the skin from a food, to whiten or soften the food, or to remove its pungent taste, or simply to bring cooking to a quick halt so that the food remains crisp rather than becoming soggy. Blanching fresh produce helps to preserve its color and flavor. To blanch vegetables, bring salted water to a rapid boil over high heat. As the water is heating, fill a large bowl three-fourths full of ice water. Carefully add the vegetables to the boiling water so that the water retains its boil. Allow the vegetables to boil until they are tender but barely cooked through. Promptly remove the vegetables from the boiling water and plunge them in the ice water. When they are no longer warm, quickly remove them from the ice bath.

blonde roux: a roux (*see* roux) made of equal amounts of fat and flour, and cooked just until the color begins to change to a pale golden color (do not brown), about 12 minutes for 1 cup of roux (1/2 cup each of fat and flour)

braising: a cooking method using both dry and moist heat, usually beginning with searing the food at a high temperature, to brown, then finishing in a covered pot. Braising can also mean cooking slowly in fat, in a covered pot with very little liquid.

caramelize: to cook until the sugar in a recipe (or a fruit or vegetable's natural sugar) liquefies to a golden to dark brown syrup, giving the recipe a nutty flavor

chiffonade: herbs or leafy vegetables cut finely or shredded, usually by stacking the leaves together, then rolling them tightly into a log or roll, and cutting thin strips off of the roll with a sharp knife. Often used as a garnish.

colander: a bowl-like utensil having holes through which water can pass, used for washing or draining solid foods

couscous: granules made of semolina wheat that is coated in finely ground wheat flour and cooked to make a cereal-like dish, often served with meat or in stews

Craisins®: a trademarked name for dried cranberries (they are technically not "craisins" unless they are produced by Ocean Spray Cranberries, Inc.; otherwise, they are simply dried cranberries)

crème fraîche: slightly soured heavy cream, sometimes used as a substitute for sour cream, though crème fraîche is thicker and not as sour. Crème fraîche is often served as a topping on desserts and fruit, or on soups and stews. It can be purchased at the store (though pricey), but is best made fresh. (See recipe, page 49.)

dark roux: a roux (*see* roux) made of equal amounts of fat (usually oil, lard, beef fat, or meat drippings) and flour, cooked to mahogany brown or near black, from twenty minutes to an hour

emulsified: blended in smoothly, of liquids that normally do not mix (e.g., oil and water)

entree: main course

file: dried, powdered sassafras leaves used to thicken soups

fines herbes: a blend of fresh herbs used to season or garnish foods, typically consisting of chervil, chives, parsley, and tarragon. Dried fines herbes can be found in many grocery stores, but are also easily prepared at home by finely mincing the herbs. Fines herbes should be added to dishes at the very end of cooking, as they lose their flavor with heat.

Framboise: a liqueur made of raspberries

Frenching: cleaning the meat from the bone

frittata: a flat omelet, sometimes baked instead of fried, and cooked with meat or vegetables

ganache: a sweet, creamy mixture made of finely chopped or grated chocolate and cream, used as a filling

Herbes de Provence: a combination of dried herbs from southern France, used mainly to add flavor to grilled meats and fish, but also used in soups and other recipes, before or during cooking. The mixture is sold in many grocery stores, but if unavailable, can be easily made at home.

Hollandaise: a rich sauce, often used as a base for other sauces, made with butter, eggs, and a vinegar reduction or lemon juice (sometimes both)

jimmies: tiny, pill-shaped candy morsels, usually chocolate or multicolored, used as a decoration on desserts; sometimes referred to as *sprinkles*

knead: to "work" with the hands, as with dough. To knead bread or biscuit dough, fold the mass of dough over and press flat with the heel of your hands several times. Kneading is best done on a lightly floured surface.

Merlot: a dry wine made from Merlot red wine grapes

mince: to chop very finely

pan-searing: See sear

pâtè: finely chopped or pureed meat or fish made into a patty, baked in a mold or a pastry, or made into a spread

phyllo: [pronounced *fee*-loh] a very thin unleavened dough that is usually layered and used to make pastries

pickling lime: food-grade calcium hydroxide powder, used in food preservation (as for pickles)

pulse: to use the pulse action of a food processor; that is, to turn on the motor for a second, then turn it off for a second, repeating until the food is blended or processed to the desired consistency

puree: to make a paste of (or a thick liquid) by grinding and/or straining until completely smooth

reduction: a thick sauce used to add flavor to recipes, made by boiling liquids (such as vinegar) until the desired volume is reached by evaporation

rémoulade: a sharp, mayonnaise-like sauce, used especially with seafood dishes *ribbon stage:* a stage reached when a whisk or spoon moved through beaten sugar and egg yolks leaves a trailing "ribbon." To achieve a perfect ribbon stage, beat the egg yolks, by hand or using an electric mixer, in a stainless steel bowl, until blended. Then add a small portion of the recipe's sugar in with the eggs and continue beating, more briskly. Gradually add the remaining sugar, beating continuously until all of the sugar has been incorporated. Beat until a small ribbon forms when some of the mixture in the bowl is dropped from a coated spoon above the surface, about three minutes by hand.

roux: (sing. or pl.) a blend of equal parts of fat (often clarified butter) and flour, cooked or browned to the desired color, and used to thicken and add flavor to soups and sauces. Roux range in color from white to almost black, based on the type of fat used and the amount of cooking time. For white, pale (blonde), or brown roux, butter (usually clarified) is often used. For a dark roux, cooks should use a fat with a high smoke point, such as canola, safflower, or soybean oil. (This allows the roux to be cooked at a higher temperature, for a shorter amount of time.) Brown roux are often made with beef fat, lard, or meat drippings. The taste of a roux will vary depending on the type of fat used.

To make a basic roux, place a saucepan on medium heat. Add 1 cup of fat to the pan (if using butter, allow it to melt); then add 1 cup of flour, stirring constantly, so the flour won't clump. Continue mixing and stirring until the roux reaches the desired color and consistency. Burnt roux or roux used in Cajun or Creole dishes are cooked anywhere from twenty minutes to an hour. For a thinner roux, use slightly less liquid. If the mixture becomes too thick, add liquid, stirring to incorporate. Once cooked, roux can be stored indefinitely in the freezer, in an airtight container. *See also* blonde roux; dark roux; white roux

rub (also dry rub*):* a blend of spices that is rubbed into meat before cooking

sauté: to fry over high heat in a small amount of fat

scald: to heat a liquid (usually milk), to just below boiling

scalloped: baked in a creamy sauce and covered with seasoned breadcrumbs

sear (or pan sear*):* to cook a food quickly at a high temperature so that only the surface is cooked. Searing meat (or fish or poultry) often causes a caramelized crust to form on the outside of the meat

simmer: to stew at or just below a boil

small dice: cut into ¼-inch cubes. To best achieve a small dice, make sure your vegetables have been washed and that your knife is sharp. Use a 6-inch non-serrated knife. Cut your vegetables first lengthwise in pieces all the same size; then gather the pieces into a bundle. Place your knife tip on the cutting board and hold it there. Begin cutting the vegetables into ¼-inch cubes by raising and lowering the handle *only*, not the knife point. Keep the tip of the knife pressed down on the cutting board. The blade will do the work, and with the knife tip held steady, you will have greater control. Your vegetables will end up diced evenly instead of chopped!

springform pan: a two-piece pan used primarily for cheesecakes, consisting of a round, flat bottom and a detachable rim that fastens with a latch. Batters or other mixtures are poured into the pan when the rim is secured onto the pan's bottom. After the food has baked, releasing the latch allows the rim to open. It can then be easily removed, and the baked good can be removed from the pan without damage. Springform pans can also be used for meatloaves, pizzas, quiches, tortes, and other types of foods that are difficult to remove from traditional bakeware.

sweat: to cook over very low heat, usually covered, until the food releases its moisture. If there are other ingredients in the pot, the flavors and juices of the sweated meat or vegetables will integrate with the other foods.

tataki: a Japanese method of preparing meat or fish that consists of brief searing over a hot flame or in a hot skillet or pan. Tataki dishes are usually briefly marinated in white or rice vinegar after searing, then sliced very thin and served with ginger ground into a paste.

temper: to bring two liquids of different temperatures to the same temperature by stirring a bit of the warmer ingredient into the cooler and blending so that the cool ingredients will mix in smoothly rather than cook solid

tempura: seafood or vegetables battered (in the traditional Japanese method, the batter often contains cornstarch) and deep-fried

terrine: an earthenware cooking dish; foods (typically meat, fish, and vegetables, chopped; or pates) cooked and served from such a dish

vinaigrette: an oil-and-vinegar–based dressing, usually seasoned with herbs and spices and used as a salad dressing or to marinate vegetables or meats

water bath: a pan of water placed into the oven to ensure that your food (for instance, in this book, a cheesecake) will bake evenly. Sometimes the bakeware in which your recipe will be cooked (for instance, a springform pan) is placed *inside* the pan of water, so it is important that interior pans are wrapped with foil so that water from the roasting pan does not leak into your recipe.

white roux: a roux (*see* roux) made of equal amounts fat and flour, and cooked just long enough to remove the floury taste, but not to change color, about 8 minutes for 1 cup of roux (1/2 cup each of fat and flour)

INDEX